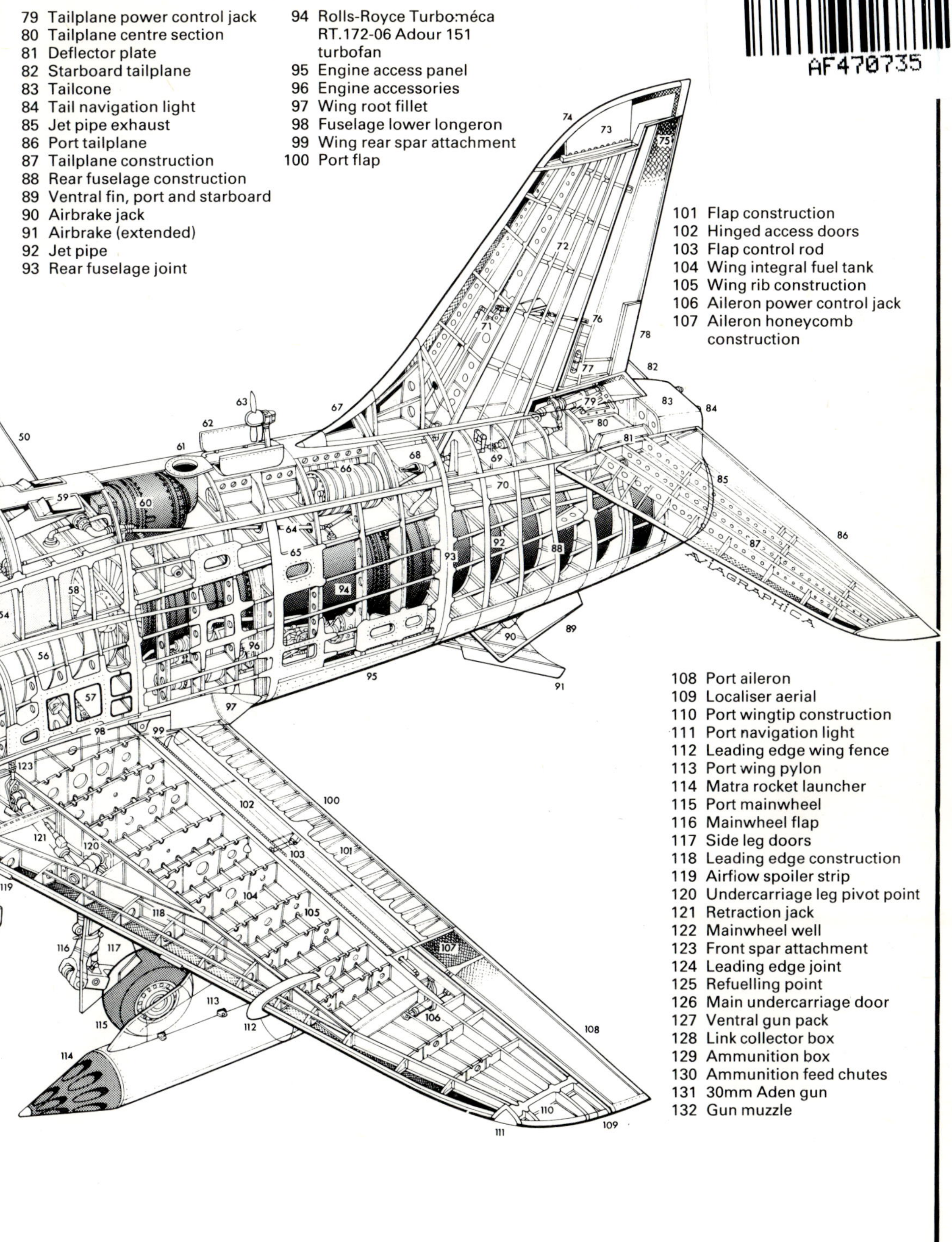

79 Tailplane power control jack
80 Tailplane centre section
81 Deflector plate
82 Starboard tailplane
83 Tailcone
84 Tail navigation light
85 Jet pipe exhaust
86 Port tailplane
87 Tailplane construction
88 Rear fuselage construction
89 Ventral fin, port and starboard
90 Airbrake jack
91 Airbrake (extended)
92 Jet pipe
93 Rear fuselage joint
94 Rolls-Royce Turboméca RT.172-06 Adour 151 turbofan
95 Engine access panel
96 Engine accessories
97 Wing root fillet
98 Fuselage lower longeron
99 Wing rear spar attachment
100 Port flap
101 Flap construction
102 Hinged access doors
103 Flap control rod
104 Wing integral fuel tank
105 Wing rib construction
106 Aileron power control jack
107 Aileron honeycomb construction
108 Port aileron
109 Localiser aerial
110 Port wingtip construction
111 Port navigation light
112 Leading edge wing fence
113 Port wing pylon
114 Matra rocket launcher
115 Port mainwheel
116 Mainwheel flap
117 Side leg doors
118 Leading edge construction
119 Airflow spoiler strip
120 Undercarriage leg pivot point
121 Retraction jack
122 Mainwheel well
123 Front spar attachment
124 Leading edge joint
125 Refuelling point
126 Main undercarriage door
127 Ventral gun pack
128 Link collector box
129 Ammunition box
130 Ammunition feed chutes
131 30mm Aden gun
132 Gun muzzle
AVIAGRAPHICA

Rona Hall and G-VTOL at Paris

BAe HAWK

Two Hawks for Zimbabwe present classic plan and side views. The far aircraft carries 190 Imp gal tanks and Sidewinders, the near one 500lb bombs. Zimbabwe did not buy either 190 Imp gal tanks nor Sidewinders, and the aircraft were on loan for this picture.

In 1980 Andy Jones, then deputy Chief Pilot of British Aerospace, Dunsfold took his Chairman, Sir Austin Pearce, on a familiarisation flight in G-HAWK. The aircraft carried Sidewinders on the inboard stations.

BAe HAWK

Arthur Reed

Contents

Acknowledgements
The author wishes to thank Andy Jones and Duncan Simpson, and the many others involved with Hawk who have helped him research this book among them Colin Chandler, Gordon Hodson, Gordon Hudson, Ralph Hooper, John Godden, Gordon Dare, Robert Gardner and John Coombs.

All the photographic and line illustrations are British Aerospace copyright unless otherwise credited.

First published 1985

ISBN 0 7110 1465 5

Published by Ian Allan Ltd, Shepperton, Surrey; and printed by Ian Allan Printing Ltd at their works at Coombelands in Runnymede, England.

1 Concept of the Warlike Trainer

In this aerospace era, designers do not leap from their baths crying 'eureka' with a revolutionary aircraft profile demanding to be inscribed upon their drawing boards. Rather a new aircraft is the product of the gradual discussion and building of ideas among a team of like-minded people over a lengthy period — which is disappointing for the writers of books on aeroplanes, for whom the eureka syndrome makes good copy. The Hawk was the product of a team, but if members of that team are pressed, they will probably agree that the moment of conception came one day during February 1968, in a hostelry in the centre of London when a small number of Hawker Siddeley Aviation people sat down for refreshment with a small number of people from the Ministry of Defence after a meeting which both sides had attended.

The HSA men had been considering among themselves what might follow the Folland Gnat and the two-seat Hawker Hunter, both ageing types, as the Royal Air Force's fast-jet trainer, and the RAF was wondering along the same lines, its ideas going so far as to include sending pilots abroad to learn part of their craft, and buying trainer aircraft offshore. At the convivial, informal occasion mentioned above, the HSA people took the opportunity to outline to their opposite numbers what they thought the next RAF trainer should be — a trainer, but something much more; a trainer with a warlike capability, particularly in the area of close support. The HSA people had come to this conclusion because they reasoned that the days when any aerospace company could afford to build a trainer aircraft tailored for one air force were, because of the costs involved, and because it would be impossible to sell it abroad, dead and gone. But give it the ability to haul weapons, then the world market could be your oyster, with the prospect of lengthy production runs and development through to the year 2000, and beyond.

Having established the dual trainer/close support idea as a basic concept, the HSA team set about allowing the aircraft to take shape. The reasoning went something along these lines — you take a pilot, and you put him in a seat; you take an instructor, and you put him in another seat, and because you want to keep the aerodynamic profile of the aircraft slim, you put the pilots in tandem, rather than side-by-side. Because you want the instructor, quite literally, to oversee the student, you put him behind and above the student; and because you want a weapon-sighting capability from the back seat, as the aircraft is also to be used in a warlike role, you put the second seat higher than it has ever been in any

Left:
Earliest public sight of the HS1182 project — which was to become the Hawk — was almost certainly this artist's impression of 1970; for a trainer, the aircraft was already being promulgated as a heavy load lifter.

other aircraft. So the reasoning went on, and out of it all emerged the shape that we know as Hawk today. The MoD people went away impressed with this novel concept of the dual-role aircraft, labelled by HSA at that time SP117, the SP standing for special project. By the middle of the following year, 1969, the SP117 had turned into P1182, and by the end of that year HSA had put a firm proposal to the MoD for consideration by, among others, a special steering committee established to consider the future of the RAF's training.

At this stage the Hawk, as it was to become, was an HSA private venture (PV) funded, with great foresight, from company finances. Costings were based on market research which assumed 300 sales world-wide. In January 1970 HSA's faith in its concept was justified when an air staff target for a fast-jet trainer with close-support capability was issued (AST 397). Encouraged by this, Hawker Siddeley increased its rate of PV spending, and in September that same year there was an official approach from MoD for cost proposals. HSA knew that the main competitor which it had to beat was a project from British Aircraft Corporation at Warton, Lancashire, the P59, built around the Rolls-Royce Viper turbojet; the Franco-West German Alpha Jet, with the Larzac turbofan, having dropped out of the running by that time. Scores of different designs were considered at the HSA factory at Kingston-upon-Thames, Surrey, and each one of these which reached the stage of being considered seriously was given a letter of the alphabet to differentiate it from the others. Thus there was an 1182A, an 1182B, and even an 1182G, which was a design based on the Gnat but which did not last long.

Engine choice produced a big in-house debate at around this time. Should the new aircraft be powered by the Rolls-Royce Viper, a tried and trusted turbo-jet, with low initial cost, but based on technology that was rapidly becoming outmoded, and nearing the end of its stretch potential, or by the Adour, a turbofan which had been developed jointly by Rolls-Royce and the French engine company Turbomeca for the Jaguar advanced trainer/low-level strike aircraft? Although more expensive in first costs, the Adour was modern in design, modular in concept, making maintenance cheap and simple, had a low fuel burn, and was capable of a lot of thrust increase for the future. A further advantage of the Adour was that it would give the RAF commonality of powerplant in both the Jaguar and the Hawk.

The HSA design team favoured the Adour, but the Viper was favoured strongly by a section of the HSA management, and a design was wrapped round a Viper and coded the 1182V. Engine choice was clouded still further by the bankruptcy of Rolls-Royce in January 1971, brought about by the company's overspending on the development of its RB211 big-fan engine for the Lockheed TriStar airliner. Then came the 1182AT, which stood for Adour trainer, but which was considered too limited in appeal for export markets looking for combat capability. This was followed by the 1182AJ, which stood for Adour for July, and which had greatly-enhanced combat performance — and this was the version which was eventually selected.

Below:
This artist's impression released in 1970 had the HS1182 in RAF training colours, a longer canopy with the instructor elevated above the pupil, but still with shoulder intakes.

Below right:
Camouflage drawing circa 1970 promoted the Hawk as a strike aircraft.

It was on 1 October 1971 that HSA heard officially that its proposal for its P1182 project, using the unreheated version of the Adour (a reheated Hawk has been considered) had been declared the winner of the competition for the RAF's new advanced jet trainer — although a war role was to be built in from the start. A competition to name the aircraft was held among HSA employees, and the winner was Tercel — a breed of Hawk. But the RAF did not much like this rather unwieldy word, and soon exchanged it for Hawk. HSA, which by that time had completed a lot of work on the view from the cockpit by building a wooden mock-up and running it up and down the runway at the company airfield at Dunsfold, Surrey on the back of a super-annuated lorry, decided to save development costs by going directly to production aircraft without any prototypes. Although the Hawk project incorporated new ideas, it was based on state-of-the-art technology, and the company knew it had the experience to jump over the prototype stage.

The main contract, signed in March 1972, was for 175 Mk 1 Hawks (176 with the first production aircraft), and the first six off the production line were earmarked to be used to test various systems and performance parameters. The first (XX154) was used for flying quality and structural load trials; the second (XX156 — there was no XX155, probably for 'cloak and dagger' reasons) was the systems aircraft and did all-weather trials; the third (XX157) performed in the spinning trials; the fourth (XX158) was the weapons aircraft; and the fifth and sixth (XX159 and XX160) went to Boscombe Down for A&AEE trials.

Having received the go-ahead from Government in early 1972, progress with the building of the early aircraft at HSA was fast and reasonably uncomplicated, and first flight took place on schedule, at Dunsfold, in August 1974. Service release came just under two years later, in July 1976, when the first two aircraft, XX161 and XX162, were delivered. Service release was on time and on cost, and to the standard required, and the RAF had spinning release from day one — unusual in a new aircraft. Five Hawk simulators ordered from Rediffusion were in place before delivery of the first aircraft. Well before the Hawk went to the RAF, word had got about among the air forces of the world that HSA was producing something rather unusual in the way of jet trainers. Early overseas interest came from Australia, and there was talk of the Hawk wing being made in that country, the RAAF seeking at that time a replacement for its Macchi 326 trainers. But nothing came of that, nor did interest from the Belgians come to fruition — in the end, they bought 33 Alpha Jets.

HSA considered that it won the contract over the competitors for the following reasons: low acquisition cost, low life-cycle cost, low risk, low fuel consumption, wide speed range, development capability, high utilisation, high reliability, high structural integrity, ease of maintenance, ease of manufacture, and export potential. HSA was also ahead of the competition because its studies had led to a very accurate definition of the aircraft, while its use of traditional costing methods and a background of experience on other projects resulted in an exceptionally accurate estimate of the overall costs involved. The studies involved were lengthy and meticulous, embracing as they did no fewer than 20 aircraft configurations and 12 engines. There were designs for tandem and side-by-side seating, swept and unswept wings, high, mid and low wings, high and low engines intakes, single or twin engines, turbofans and turbojets.

A lot of time was spent in analysing the good and poor aspects of the existing jet trainer aircraft of the time, and in establishing in great detail the airborne task of what was to become the Hawk. The HSA submission for the Ministry of Defence competition included the manufacture and testing of low-speed, $\frac{1}{2}$-scale, and one-tenth wind-tunnel models. Work was also carried out on a one-thirteenth scale high-speed model.

Mr Gordon Hodson, one of the original HSA Hawk design team at Kingston, recalled those heady days in a paper which he gave to the Royal Aeronautical Society in London in 1983. The incentives to establish reliable cost estimates were high, he said, due to a competitive environment, the prize of a large number of Royal Air Force aircraft, and considerable export potential. The contract was fixed-price for the design, development and manufacture of the 176 Mk 1 aircraft, and this included the meeting of the requirements of AvP 970, entitled *Design Requirements for Aircraft of the Royal Air Force and Royal Navy*, and an acceptance standard agreed between the Ministry of Defence (Procurement Executive) and HSA. All aircraft were to be built using production tooling, and the programme included full ground and flight tests, to be verified by the Royal Aircraft Establishment (RAE), Farnborough, and the Aircraft and Armament Experimental Establishment (A&AEE), Boscombe Down. The acceptance standard defined demonstrations of technical achievement, and included 11 aircraft

Above:
By 1971, as shown by this wind tunnel model, the tailplane had been sloped and extended, and three small wing fences had appeared.

Above right:
Final design began to emerge in this artist's drawing circa 1972, with the engine intakes dropped from shoulder to wing height.

Right:
Gordon Hodson, one of the leaders of the HSA team which fathered the Hawk, holds what appears to be the definitive design in this 1972 picture. Mr Hodson later headed the British Aerospace drive to sell the Hawk to the US Navy.

performance guarantees, all of which were either equalled or exceeded.

The fixed-price contract defined the project as contractor furnished equipment (CFE), with one exception — the Adour engine, which was Government furnished equipment (GFE). This allowed HSA direct access to the equipment suppliers, and gave the opportunity to establish long-term business agreements, and a firm data base for export negotiation. It was recognised that the Hawk must have development and export potential, and it was therefore agreed between MoD and HSA to include in the contract specification the statement that 'the design shall be capable of conversion to a close-support role using one centre-line pylon and two

outer-wing pylons, including the carriage of jettison-able external fuel tanks, heavy weapons and twin-stores carriers. The close-support potential was to have minimum effect on the efficiency of the aircraft in its training role'. This led to the successful development by BAe of the Hawk's attack role.

Subsequent amendments were made to the contract for maintenance incentives and reliability incentives. The maintenance incentives were directed to ensure low life-cycle costs, and this was achieved by specifying target times for maintenance activities. A total of 95 maintenance activities were specified. To give some examples: for pre-flight servicing the contract specified 15 man-minutes, and HSA demonstrated it in 12.8. The times for turn-round servicing were 15/8.8; post-flight servicing, 35/33.5; re-arming gunpod and two pylons, 60/37.3; engine change, 500/369; replace ejection seat, 240/42.3; replace UHF radio, 15/5.5; replace battery, 15/7. Average time to replace or change 95 specified items, such as control column handle or aileron trim actuator, was 90/57.8. Demonstration of the 95 actions was made under controlled conditions. All the contract base lines were achieved except two, 'and to the delight of the Royal Air Force, and Treasury's surprise, HSA was paid the maximum money allowed in the contract'.

Mr Hodson said that the reliability incentives were established to ensure high reliability of operation when the aircraft entered Royal Air Force service. Targets were set for the maximum acceptable number of defects per flying hour on a range of airframe and equipment items. Two years after the Hawk had entered RAF service, the defects occurring in 2,000 flying hours at the Advanced Flying School, and 1,000 flying hours at the Tactical Weapons Unit, were assessed. The achieved defect rate per flying hour was significantly lower than the contractual base rate, and a further substantial payment was made to HSA.

Service experience had continued to demonstrate the reliability of the Hawk. Up to early 1984 no aircraft had been lost due to technical failure, with the total flying hours exceeding 200,000. Hawk operations had shown that the defect rates and maintenance support were at a more economic level than previously experienced. In addition to providing savings of money and manpower in service, the demonstrated achievements showed that planned investments for spares and support funding could be estimated with confidence, leading to more effective and efficient aircraft utilisation. Throughout the development programme, regular design and production meetings were held at HSA and MoD(PE). No change to the design was made without full justification related to the technical requirement and the terms of the contract. All aspects of the programme were recorded and reported at regular intervals, and the acceptance standard demonstration reports were forwarded to MoD(PE) for approval. Where there were differences of opinion, agreement was reached on action to be taken after negotiation between the two sides.

Factors relating to the success achieved on the Hawk project were, Mr Hodson said, the definition of the project in good detail before cost estimates were commenced; the maximum use of known technology; the starting of wind tunnel tests early in the programme; a firm background of previous aircraft cost performance, technical data and operational aspects; a thorough understanding of the operational task; opportunity to report cost estimates to the design and production engineers; a competitive environment; strong commercial incentives (176 aircraft for the RAF, and a large export potential); use of an existing engine; use of known and proven equipment; one contract — production aircraft were not ordered in batches; no prototype aircraft — production tooling was used from the beginning; rigid project control within HSA, MoD, and MoD(PE) to ensure all project aspects were justified; and great enthusiasm and dedication for the project to succeed.

'It would be untrue to say there were no problems, but it is true to say there were no major problems', Mr Hodson stated. 'The problems encountered were typical of those expected when co-ordinating the many disciplines and components of a modern, fast jet military aircraft.' He added:

'Success (of the Hawk programme) is a firm base for the future. The aircraft's capabilities are being extended, allowing additional roles to be achieved. Export potential is considerable, and the Hawk will see service in the world's air forces well into the 21st century. Finally, it is of interest to note that wherever there has been fair competition, the Hawk has won. Since the original 1971 MoD competition, the Hawk has won seven more, the most significant being the selection, on 19 November, 1981, of a Hawk-based system, in conjunction with McDonnell Douglas (Douglas Aircraft Company) and Sperry Systems for development as the United States Navy's new jet trainer aircraft to be part of the VTXTS training system (which is planned to be operational with the Hawk T45 during the late 1980s, and which requires at least 300 aircraft)'.

Below:
1972 in the experimental shop at Hawker Siddeley Aircraft, Kingston. In the foreground is the full scale mock-up/space model in which all the cockpit layouts and installations were planned.

2 Hawk Description and Construction

A general description of the Hawk Mk 1 is that it is a low-wing monoplane of conventional layout, powered by a single Rolls-Royce Turbomeca Adour Mk 151 turbofan engine. The fuselage is of conventional construction, being built up of frames, stringers and metal skin, while the wing is moderately swept and built in one piece. It is attached to the fuselage by six bolts, the centre section of the wing running through a cut-out in the base of the fuselage. Most of the main wing box forms a large integral fuel tank, and the main landing gear retracts inwards and forwards ahead of the main box. Ailerons and slotted flaps are mounted on the trailing edge of the wing.

The equipment is situated in the fuselage with a view to ease of accessibility and maintenance, and the aircraft is designed to have a high reliability, a low mean time to repair failures, and minimum

Above:
Fine plan view of G-HAWK shows clearly how the advanced wing section which Hawker Siddeley Aviation designed allows the use of a modest sweep angle, which in turn permits the stores to be on the centre of gravity — so avoiding handling problems, and severe limits on outboard stores. The military registration ZA101 is used when G-HAWK is on warlike exercises.

scheduled servicing. Equipment and systems are designed for a long fatigue life. The canopy covering the two tandem cockpits is built in one piece and opens sideways, hinging from the right, while the windscreen is also in one piece in stretched acrylic, and hinges forward to facilitate servicing of the flight instruments. It is of single curvature and provides good visibility in rain. Cabin conditioning is provided by a system utilising engine bleed air installed to give pressurisation and temperature control — cabin pressurisation is provided automatically. Temperature control is also automatic, following pilot selection of the desired level. Manual override is available in the event of malfunction of the automatic system.

During normal operation, 80% of the incoming air is directed at the aircrew, with the remaining air passing over the transparencies. However, when 'demist' is selected, this is reversed, and 80% of the flow is directed over the transparencies. A great deal of care was taken in design to give both pupil and instructor as wide a field of view as possible. The instructor has been raised in order that he may have a downward view of 6° straight ahead to enable him to demonstrate weapon firing and release from the rear cockpit. Much care was also taken in the layout of the front and rear pilot stations, not only with the placing of the flying controls and equipment, but in the selection of modern instruments.

Each pilot has a Martin Baker Type 10 ejector seat, basically common to that used in the Tornado multi-role combat aircraft. No delay is incorporated in firing the seat, the pilots ejecting through the canopy, which is shattered automatically by a miniature detonating cord running round the periphery, with an additional overhead pattern. Either seat can be fired individually, or the instructor can initiate the firing of both seats in sequence. If command ejection is used, there is half a second delay between the seats firing, and the rocket thrust diverges slightly to ensure that the seats do not collide after they have left the aircraft. If the instructor or captain of the aircraft should occupy the front seat, suitable arrangements are made to isolate the command ejection sequence on the ground before take-off.

The ailerons and one-piece tailplane are hydraulically powered, and feel is provided by spring feel units. Trim is provided by biasing the zero datum on the spring feel unit electrically, and additional stick force per G is provided by means of a bob weight. The ailerons and tailplane are both actuated by tandem power-operated jacks, each half being supplied by separate hydraulic systems. There is no manual reversion, but a ram-air turbine is provided to supply to the flying controls should engine seizure, or No 2 hydraulic pump failure, occur. The rudder is non-powered and directional trim is by means of a simple, electrically-driven trim tab. Duplicated hydraulic systems working at 3,000lb/sq in provide power for the tailplane, ailerons, flaps, airbrake, undercarriage and the anti-skid wheel brakes.

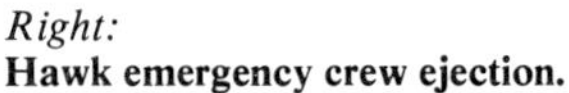

Right:
Hawk emergency crew ejection.

Left:
Detail of Hawk canopy. The green flag under the windscreen indicates to the ground crew that the pilot has selected weapon systems to 'safe'.

The No 1 hydraulic system provides power to one section of the tandem jacks operating ailerons and tailplane, in addition to the other hydraulic services. In the event of loss of system pressure, the undercarriage, flaps and wheel brakes can be operated by accumulators charged with compressed nitrogen. The No 2 system provides power to the other section of the flying control tandem jacks. An accumulator maintains pressure during the interval between the failure of the primary power source and the extension of the ram air turbine. Electrical power is obtained from a single 28volt 9kW brushless dc generator. The unit is mounted on the engine accessory gearbox, and is cooled by an internal fan, and by ram air. Two 18amp hour Type J batteries are fitted, and these provide emergency power in the event of malfunction of the main supply. AC power is derived from two 500VA static inverters, providing general service main and standby supply.

The Hawk is capable of operating on either Avtur or Avtag, and the fuel is carried in one flexible bag tank installed in the centre fuselage, and in one integral tank in each wing. Tank capacities are: fuselage tank, 818litre (180 Imp gal); wing tanks, 795litre (175 Imp gal); and drop tanks (optional on wing inboard pylons) 455litre each (100 Imp gal) or 590litre (130 Imp gal) or 860litre (190 Imp gal). Fuel transfers first from the fuselage tank, and then from the wing tanks to a collector tank in the wing centre box. It is then fed to the engine by an electrically-powered booster pump. A double-entry pump is fitted for negative G conditions, and there is sufficient capacity for up to 30 seconds inverted flight at maximum fuel flow. The aircraft can be recovered in safety following either the failure of the fuel system pressurisation, or of the fuel booster pump. Gravity and single-point pressure refuelling facilities are provided.

The Rolls-Royce Turbomeca Adour Mk 151 turbofan in the Hawk Mk 1 has a bypass ratio of 0.9, and develops a sea-level static thrust of 5,340lb under ISA conditions. The Adour is of modular construction, so that any module can be incorporated without the need to rebalance the rotating assemblies. The engine is of the two-spool type, with the low-pressure assembly comprising a two-stage fan driven by a single-stage turbine, and the high-pressure spool having five compressor stages, again driven by a single-stage turbine. A fully-annular combustion chamber is employed. The bypass air annulus which surrounds the engine keeps casing temperatures, and the jet pipe surface temperature, low so that fire risk is reduced. An integral gas turbine starter, using engine fuel, is used. Engine access and removal is by way of large doors beneath the engine.

The Hawk may look a simple, straightforward aeroplane, but its manufacturing process involves the skills of thousands of men and women working within British Aerospace and their suppliers, and can take up to two years from the time that long-lead items are ordered to the moment when the finished product, resplendent in the colours of the customer, is signed over by one of BAe's test pilots as being fit for delivery and entry into service.

Four BAe factories are involved in Hawk production. Kingston, Surrey produces the cockpit section and engine intakes, and part of the nose; Brough, Yorkshire the centre fuselage section, the wing and moving surfaces, the fin, the tailplane and the rudder; Hamble, Hampshire the cockpit canopy, the centre aft fuselage, the rear fuselage and part of the nose section; and Dunsfold, Surrey installs the systems, carries out final assembly, paints the aircraft, test flies them and does the delivery flight and hand-over.

Production is a mixture of conventional techniques and advanced technology, and for ease of manufacture the structure is divided into convenient sections to allow access by operators through all the assembly stages. This form of structural breakdown also simplifies work-sharing, and is suitable for either large or small-quantity manufacture.

The structure of the Hawk consists primarily of aluminium alloys, and a high proportion of these are in sheet form. The wing incorporates integral fuel tanks, and is formed of skins, ribs and spars machined from aluminium alloy slabs, delivered to the factory from the metal mills in roughly-shaped billets. A small number of fuselage parts are also machined from aluminium alloy slabs. Attachment fittings, hinge fittings and points of load concentration are generally machined from aluminium alloy or steel, while heat shields, and a few other parts, are manufactured in titanium.

Traditional capstan and turret lathes, milling and drilling machines, and grinding and broaching machines are employed, but there are also a number of NC (numerically-controlled) milling machines, and plugboard-controlled turning machines. The metal skins of the Hawk are formed by stretch forming, drop hammer forming, and rolling. The main structural breakdown in manufacturing stages is as follows: nose and cockpit, centre fuselage, wing, rear fuselage, tailplane and fin.

The front fuselage section includes the cockpits for both pilots, and provision for the later attachment of the nose undercarriage, canopy and windscreen, pilots' seats, flying controls, avionics equipment and

landing light. The structure breaks down into major sub-assemblies consisting of the front floor structure, nose cone, rear floor structure, port and starboard side structures and the structure below the rear floor. These are brought together in two assembly fixtures to produce a complete front fuselage structure, which is then pressure tested and painted internally prior to the installation of systems forward of the rear seat frame. This work is completed at Dunsfold, prior to mating with the centre fuselage, and for ease of access during installation the nose section of the fuselage is mounted on a rotatable jig.

The forward portion of the centre fuselage contains the fuselage fuel tank, which is located just behind the rear cockpit seat. The tank is flexible, and is attached to the inside walls and the tank roof by

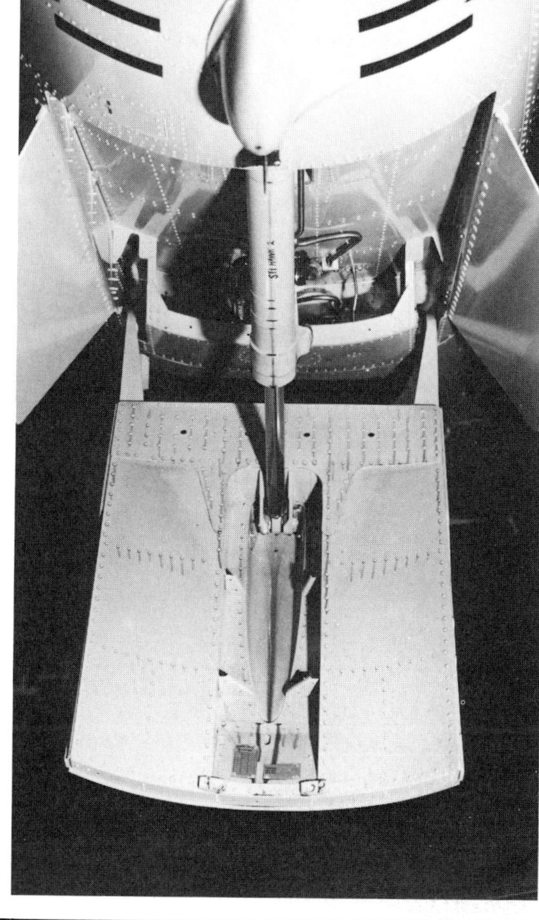

Hawk main dimensions

Overall length: 11.96m (39.2ft)
Span: 9.4m (30.83ft)
Height: 4.1m (13.4ft)
Wing area: 16.7sq m (180sq ft)
Thickness/chord ratio (root): 10.9%
Thickness/chord ratio (tip): 9%
Leading edge sweep: 26°
Quarter chord sweep: 21.5°
Internal fuel: 1,360kg (3,000lb); 1,705litre (375 Imp gal); 450 US gal
External fuel: Up to 380 Imp gal (460 US gal)
Stressing limits with full fuel: +8G, −4G
Stressing limits with 1,360kg (3,000lb) external stores, plus 60% internal fuel: +8G, −4G
Trainer take-off mass: 5,035kg (11,100lb)
Max take-off mass: 8,350kg (18,405lb)

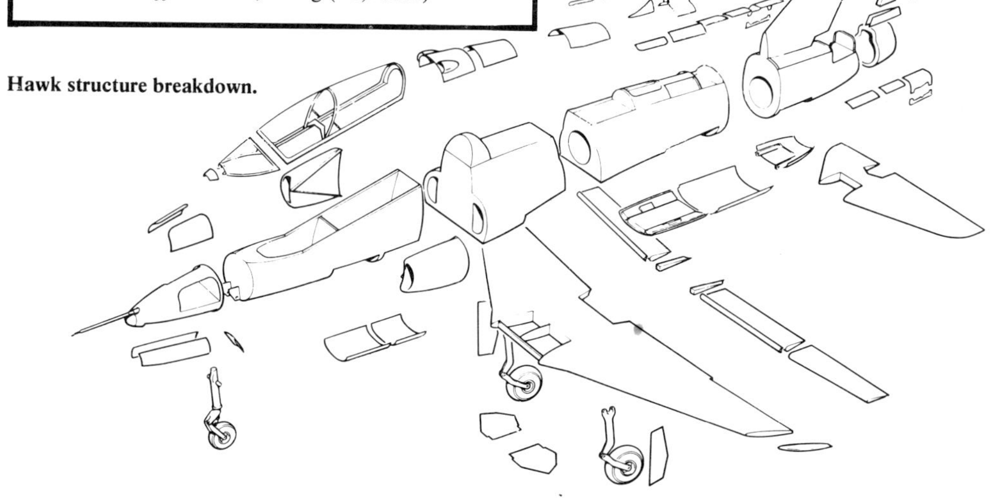

Hawk structure breakdown.

special fasteners. The inside shape of this box is complicated by the presence of the engine air intakes built into the side of the structure. The section also carries the six wing attachment fittings. Built into the aft portion of the centre fuselage are the mounting points, accessibility and removal points for the Adour engine. The portion contains four sub-assemblies — the engine mounting structure (forward), the engine mounting assembly (aft), the side structure (port), and the side structure (star-board). Titanium is used in this section for the main upper diaphragms for engine mountings; the remainder is aluminium. Conventional riveting and bolting is employed for the structure, and the exter-nal skin is attached with countersunk aluminium alloy rivets.

The rear fuselage carries the mountings for the fin, airbrake, airbrake operating jack and the tailplane powered-control unit, and the section also has all the fittings for the engine tailpipe installation. Again, this section is primarily aluminium, riveted and bolted, but mushroom head rivets are used externally because of the thin skins in the section. The top area of the section is formed of panels for access to the equipment bays. Access panels and removable doors are made as separate components to inter-changeability standards. Water sealant is applied to all door surrounds, and the internal fuselage structure in the engine area is painted in white gloss.

Port and starboard air intakes are built as separate pieces, as they attach to both the front and centre fuselage sections, and can only be conveniently fitted after these two sections are joined together. The intakes are not designed to be detachable and inter-changeable, but they are replaceable in the event of damage.

The centre fuselage forward section is joined to the centre fuselage aft/rear sections in a mating fixture, completion of the join being made with the assistance of supporting trestles. The front fuselage is then rolled forward on a mating trolley, and the two units are bolted together. At this stage the intakes and the fin are attached.

The wing of the Hawk is a single piece, full-span structure with two main spars which, with upper and lower skin panels, from integral fuel tanks. Another spar forms the additional support for the main under-carriage mounting, the undercarriage itself retracting inwards. The wing consists of six sub-assemblies — the inner leading edge (port and starboard), the outer leading edge (port and starboard) and the wing tip (port and starboard). Wings for the Hawk are made in two distinct stages, firstly when they are built up in a vertical fixture, and secondly when the structure is completed in a horizontal fixture. All systems, including the undercarriage and flaps, are installed, functioned and adjusted, so reducing the need for additional testing when the entire unit arrives at Dunsfold for joining to the fuselage.

The BAe Hamble factory, where Hawk windscreens and canopies are made, is specially-suited to this work because, with the advent of stretched acrylic, creep-forming techniques were developed there in the early 1970s. Hamble produces a wind-screen with good impact resistance which, at the same time, retains the grade one optical qualities necessary for weapon-sighting head-up-display instrumentation. Hamble also carried out further development work in canopy manufacture to meet Hawk requirements for a large arc of vision for both crew members, and fully-mechanised techniques are now employed for manufacturing these large shells to a high optical standard.

The shell is formed of three pieces, forward and rear sections being made of acrylic, and the centre of terylene/acrylic laminate, which acts as a join between them, and also as the attachment of the rear windscreen. The shell is secured in a metallic structural framework, hinging along its starboard side. Each shell is separately heat-moulded, as is the centre section. The three parts are then trimmed and bonded, and terylene laminate edge-reinforcing members are fitted. After completion the shell is annealed in an oven to remove stresses due to forming operations. The shell is held in an open-type fixture, which is also used for final edge trimming. Temperature, time and cleanliness are strictly con-

Above:
Detail of Hawk's nosewheel and undercarriage. The anchor on strut indicates strong point.

trolled during these operations, Hamble's ovens being controllable to closer than 1°C, and fully instrumented.

After trimming, the canopy and its supporting framework are mated, and the associated equipment, including the locking mechanism, ejection system and demist pipes, are fitted. The windscreen is then attached. This consists of a one-piece, stretched, high-strength acrylic shell contained in a metal frame, the entire section pivoting forward to provide access to the forward instrument panel. A neoprene rubber seal around the edge of the shell is secured by retaining plates. The completed unit is then pressure-tested.

The tailplane is a one-piece aerofoil which attaches to the fuselage at two hinges, about which it can

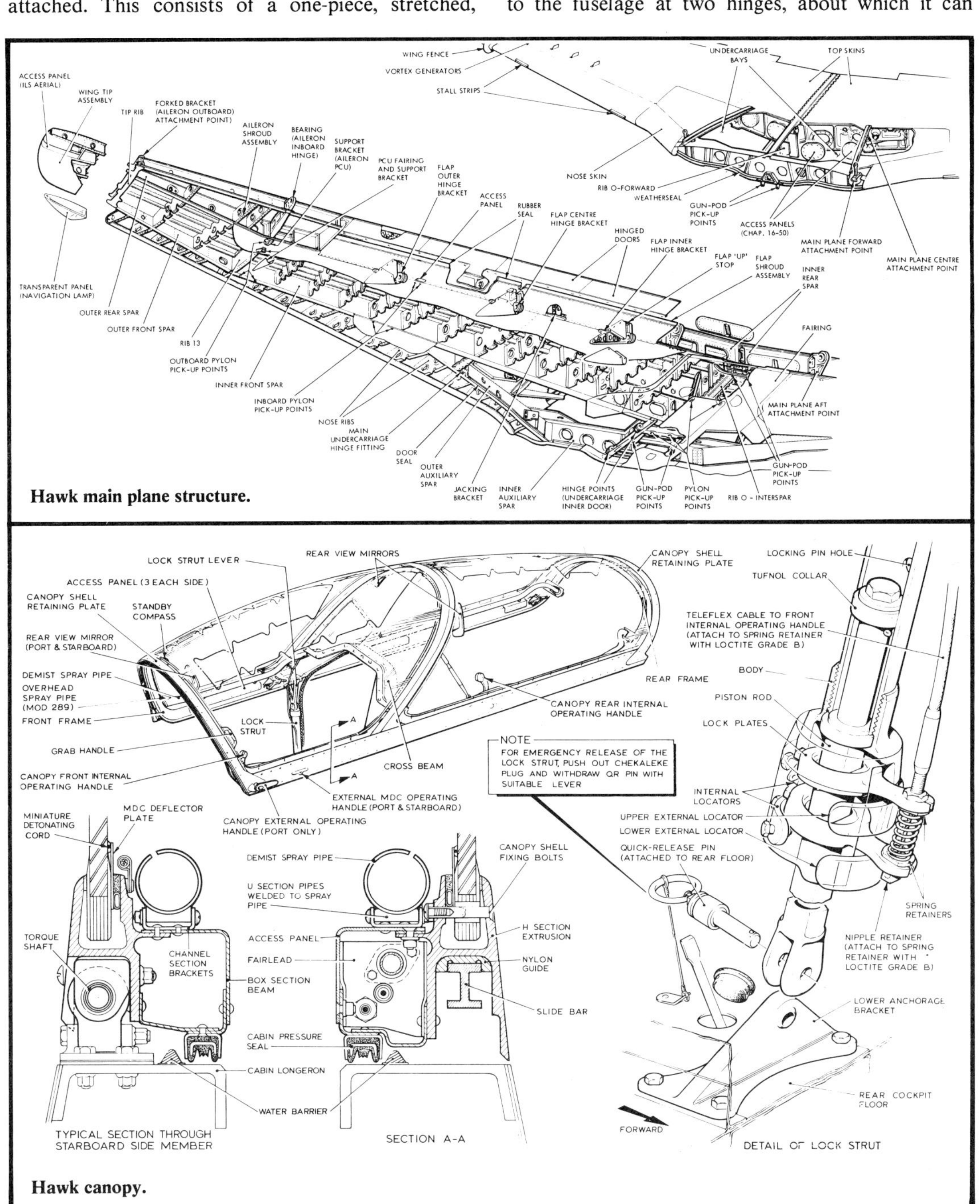

Hawk main plane structure.

Hawk canopy.

pivot under the movement of a powered-control unit. The main skin panels on the top and bottom surfaces are numerically-control machined and are joined at the centreline with heavy butt-straps. The fin consists of front and rear spars, ribs and stiffeners, all covered with chemically-etched skins. Assembly of the complete unit is carried out in one fixture, which controls all the interchangeability points. The fixture is designed to hold the fin in the vertical attitude, with the leading edge downwards. The tailcone, which forms the detachable portion of the rear fuselage, is made from light alloy apart from one frame and the rear cone, which are welded from titanium sub-assemblies. Assembly is carried out in one fixture. The airbrake consists of a riveted light alloy structure of diaphragms, inner and outer skins, with hinge members machined from light alloy forgings (the single airbrake on the basic Hawk design is replaced by two on the version for the United States Navy).

Some of the sections of the Hawk made at other BAe factories arrive at Dunsfold for final assembly already 'stuffed' with systems. The units of the electrical and avionics systems are mainly located in the forward equipment bay and below the rear pilot's

Below:
Hawk's ram air turbine pops up from a hatch on its back just forward of the fin. Starter exhaust port is in foreground.

floor, necessitating the provision of cables connecting these bays with the instrument panels and consoles at the two pilots' stations, and to points throughout the aircraft, including the radio aerials, and the five weapon pylon positions.

Independent wiring is provided for armament control circuits, but many individual leads are grouped into cable assemblies, and convenient breaks are provided with plug and socket connectors for ease of assembly. Cable looms are made up from individual wires, with crimped type joints at the plug and socket connectors, and the electrical system includes in addition, a number of junction and control boxes incorporating internal wiring which are made up as separate units. Pre-assembly of cable harnesses in the front fuselage is carried out on fixtures representing the aircraft structure, and these are capable of being transferred directly to the aircraft, with the minimum of time required for installation.

Sections arrive at Dunsfold on low-loader road vehicles, and the final assembly, painting and test-flying phases are completed there. Assembly of the installations into the fuselage is carried out in a series of stages, each identified for computer control of stock, using kits of parts previously grouped in the stores. Adour engines are sent directly from Rolls-Royce at Derby to Dunsfold. Mated fuselages and other parts are placed in a special rig which rotates them to make sure that no foreign objects, such as tools and pieces of metal, have been left inside during manufacture. This operation is carried out when the factory is quiet, so that inspectors are able to hear any giveaway 'clunking' noises as the rig turns slowly.

Each stage of installation is progressively cleared by inspection in accordance with stage instructions, and clearance is recorded on aircraft history cards. Overall clearance of most systems is carried out at a function stage after the wing and tail units are fitted, and installations are complete. Avionics equipment, and ejection seats (which are unsuitable for fitting in the initial stages), are fitted and cleared at stages immediately prior to first flight. The aircraft are painted in yellow primer, and are generally test-flown in this condition, the paint being touched up, and then covered by the customer's livery just before delivery.

Meanwhile, back at Kingston factory, two Hawks do vital service on the ground. One is fitted with an experimental cockpit, and is used to test lighting and other systems against BAe and customer requirements. The other, an early T Mk 1 model, which has never flown is in a test rig having its airframe structure 'tortured' with constant strains and stresses, while wired up to strain gauges, so building up thousands of test hours, and proving the reliability of the structures of the hundreds of Hawks which are in service with air forces all over the world.

3 Developing a Family of Aircraft

The Hawk has few, if any vices, and the only excitements which it produces for its pilots are nice ones. Although not designed to be supersonic, it soon went through the sound barrier in a dive and eventually achieved a true Mach number of around 1.2, where its Machmeter now has a stop. The aircraft does not in fact have a handling limit as far as speed is concerned, but is limited by its drag — if you take it up to its maximum altitude and point its nose vertically at the ground, there comes a point where it just will not go downhill any faster.

So viceless is the Hawk that there are a few who have opined that it is too 'well-behaved' to be a successful trainer, and that students need a little more uncertainty, or 'bite' to put them on their mettle. But this view is dismissed by most experienced pilots who have flown it. They take the view that the Hawk behaves so like a modern combat aircraft in the broad spectrum of its flight envelope — its range, endurance, speed, manoeuvrability and the G it pulls, that this stretches the student sufficiently. Modern air forces, they point out, are no longer in the business of operating aircraft that are 'difficult' to fly.

Unlike some other trainers, the Hawk will not depart from the stall unless it is commanded to do so. Instead, it shudders and shakes to indicate that the speed is too low, and instructors are able to demonstrate the effects of gross mishandling, and to invite their students to make mistakes with safety. The designers of the Hawk 'got it right' in a big way, injecting into it a lot of experience garnered in producing the aerodynamics of the Harrier, Hunter, Gnat and Sea Hawk. Such experience was beginning to become rather rare when the Hawk was on the drawing board, for design teams in aerospace

Below:
On its first Middle East tour during January and February 1978, G-HAWK shows off its load-carrying potential over inhospitable territory. Picture was taken in Masira from a Strikemaster of the Sultanate of Oman Air Force.

industries all over the world had been concentrating heavily on producing faster and faster supersonics, and the art of sculpting shapes which were not only good to fly but which did not cost a fortune to buy and then operate had been partially forgotten. One of the great successes of the Hawk design is the wing which looks simple but is not, and which results in the single Adour engine pushing six tons of aircraft along with a fuel burn of only 4,500lb/hr, while heavyweight supersonic fighters drink up to 15 times as much. A further advantage of the single Adour configuration is that it gives out a very low infra-red signature. Simulation has shown that up against a high-powered fighter using afterburner, Hawk would have a head-on missile-firing opportunity at the beginning of the comabt which the opponent would lack.

The fact that Hawker Siddeley was given what amounted to a blank piece of paper when it came to the design of the equipment which was to go into the Hawk has, in the view of the pilots, resulted in an aircraft which is uncomplicated, easy to maintain, and is not prey to accidents caused by technical snags. The pilot's actions on control column and rudder pedals are, for instance, communicated to the moving surfaces through push rods. Cables and pulleys as used in earlier aircraft were discarded on the grounds that they were difficult to maintain, cables stretched, and foreign objects tended to lodge in the system. Hawk was given a duplicated hydraulic system with no manual reversion, but the ram-air turbine as back-up in cases of complete failure gives those who fly the aircraft a welcome 'insurance policy'.

The team of development pilots were able, during often-lengthy debates, to have their proposals built into the detailed design of the aircraft — although not every one of their suggestions was accepted. One of their particular achievements was a pair of cockpits roomy enough to accommodate with comfort colleagues with exceptionally long legs. The rightness of the basic design which emerged from those early discussions may be judged by the fact that it has not been found necessary to alter it, except in small detail, over a decade, unless it was to extend the aircraft's capability.

One of the great attractions of the Hawk in the training role is its tandem cockpit layout with the rear — instructor's — seat set considerably higher than that of the student in front. This was a relatively new concept at the time of the Hawk design, most trainers before that having been designed in tandem, but both instructor and pupil sitting at about the same level, with obvious restrictions to the former's view, or side-by-side, in which case the view of either crewman was, 'all left, or all right'. Hawk's cockpit was laid out with four basic parameters in mind: 1 — to give both pilots an unrestricted view of the runway on the approach to land; 2 — to give them a

Above:

In 1977 G-HAWK/ZA101 was engaged in trials with the Hunting Engineering BL755 cluster bomb. The weapons are painted black and white so that they will show up on the trials photographs.

Below:

Wearing brown and sand camouflage, the demonstrator Hawk was engaged in rocket projectile trials at Pembry during 1978.

good forward view during low flying, such as fast runs through the Welsh valleys; 3 — to give them a good view for ground-attack manoeuvres, with weapon sight duplicated in the rear seat; and 4 — to give as good a view as possible for formation flying and for combat training.

As a result, the rear-seat man does not spend his time staring at the back of the front-seat man's head, but sees over him through his own windscreen in the large canopy. This staggered seating arrangement also gives the instructor the facility to see something of what his student is doing, and the duplicated controls in the rear cockpit tell him the rest of the story. In size the Hawk cockpits are fairly generous, and certainly bigger than those of the Lighting, Harrier and Mirage 3. As one Hawk pilot put it, 'The student certainly doesn't feel he is in a kiddie car when he climbs into the aircraft — more that he is in a fighter-size aeroplane.' Comment from pilots who have been used to flying US, Soviet, German, French and UK fast jets on their first contact with the Hawk is summed up in an often-repeated phrase 'I feel at home in this aircraft.' To employ the US vernacular, the Hawk is one of those machines which is, 'user-friendly'.

The Hawk is unlimited in terms of Mach number at high level in training sorties, with or without gun or pylon stores, and its maximum speed at low level is 575kt, although the RAF reduces this figure to 550kt. The aircraft is cleared to 8G, but it has been demonstrated to 9G, with a maximum of 9.3G during trials. At one time the aircraft was considered for use in the development of a high G fighter cockpit, which would have meant it being cleared up to 10G without shortening the life of the airframe, but that project was cancelled. The aircraft is cleared up to minus 4G.

Each of the five hard points beneath the Hawk — one on the fuselage centreline, and two on either wing — is designed to carry a nominal 1,000lb, a total of 5,000lb (aircraft weight empty is 8,000lb). The 1,000lb figure is at plus 8G, and during trials it proved possible to carry as much as 2,000lb on a single station, albeit at a lower G limitation. The Hawk has been flown with a total of 6,800lb of external stores. The aircraft has been cleared to 8G carrying 3,000lb of external stores, and to 5.5G with 5,000lb. All stores configurations have been cleared

Below:
Payload for G-HAWK in this 1977 picture consisted of a centreline 250lb bomb, drop tanks with fins on the inboard pylons, and Matra pods on the outers.

Above:
Black and white paint job on new-style finless fuel tanks in 1977 indicates that they were ready for drop tests from G-HAWK.

Right:
First flight of G-HAWK, the HSA private venture demonstrator, was from Dunsfold on 17 May 1976, and in this picture Duncan Simpson is strapping in. Aircraft was initially painted in desert camouflage, indicating the area of the world where HSA hoped for sales.
BAe via Duncan Simpson

Far right:
At the time of writing this was the heaviest load that Hawk had carried — four 1,000lb and four 500lb bombs, in 1978.

to Mach 0.8 number, or 500kt. Inevitably, the Hawk is affected by the drag of external stores, but even with four 1,000lb bombs hanging beneath it, plus a gun pod on the centreline, it still turns in a maximum sea-level speed of 500kt.

Because the stores sit close to the longitudinal centre of gravity, the handling of the aircraft while it is hauling heavy loads is not greatly affected, and it is still possible to stall it and produce the same characteristics as the trainer in a clean configuration. It has, in fact, been proved in trials that even when the Hawk is carrying up to its own weight, it is still not seriously affected from the points of view of either speed or handling.

Many of the parameters mentioned above have been proved through the use of the company aircraft registered G-HAWK, number seven off the Dunsfold assembly line, which over the years has been worked hard with trials of every piece of kit imaginable, from stores-carrying, through instrument trials, to gun-firing, while, in between, visiting almost every quarter of the globe in search of fresh sales. G-HAWK is a British Aerospace private venture, with not a penny of Government funding involved — in fact, at the time of writing, the British taxpayer has received back around £20million as a result of Hawk airframe sales overseas, and probably a similar amount by way of Rolls-Royce through sales of the Adour. Also at the time of writing, Rolls had taken programme leadership on the Adour — originally developed for the Jaguar programme — with Turbomeca, the French manufacturer, providing parts under sub-contract.

From its original conception in the mid-1960s, the Hawk has developed, in a somewhat piecemeal way rather than to any great master plan, into a whole 'family' of aircraft — a family that looks as if it will go on growing right through into the 21st century. Of its contemporaries, probably only the F-5 has had a similar progressive success. The main reasons for Hawk's longevity are twofold: the rightness of the basic design; and the fact that it entered the aerospace scene during the 1970s when, because of the world fuel crisis, there was a great incentive for manufacturers and air forces to capitalise on what they had got, rather than to pour buckets of money into brand-new concepts.

Although envisaged at first as a trainer, Hawk has turned into a truly multi-role aeroplane, capable of performing roles which include close air-support, reconnaissance, interdiction, barrier air defence, maritime, and possibly anti-helicopter operations.

For an aircraft of its small size it has demonstrated phenomenal load-carrying capabilities, hauling five 1,000lb bombs 300nm on a low/low sortie, and twice that distance at high level. Hawk could, it is thought, carry 10,500lb of disposable load, and could even increase that by a further 1,500lb with a touch more thrust tweaked into its Adour. The Hawk has also benefited from the fact that its development period has paralleled the immense breakthrough of the microchip, and consequent miniaturisation, enabling to be packed into it for general data management, black boxes which, when the aircraft was first thought of, would have been so big that they would have required a furniture van to move them, and a team of six or seven men to operate them.

Weapons development has also marched side by side with Hawk so that it now has potential for carrying all manner of 'smart' devices, the flagship among which is undoubtedly the Sea Eagle anti-ship missile, already demonstrated on Hawk's centreline station. Hawks could carry other similar missiles which are coming along the development path. Carrying Sea Eagle, and fitted with a pair of 190 Imp gal fuel tanks underwing, Hawk has a radius of action of over 800nm. In such a configuration it would be possible to use it, at modest cost, to help close the gap to the Soviet Navy between northwest Britain and Iceland.

In the meantime, Hawk users are offered a bewildering choice of underwing hardware, from various types of rockets in pods, bombs of all types — 250lb, 500lb and 1,000lb (an aircraft has carried a maximum of four 500lb and four 1,000lb, plus a centreline gun) — machine gun, or 30mm Aden cannon (the projected single-seater will carry inboard two 25mm cannon of the type being produced for the Harrier). Three external fuel tanks are in the inventory — 100, 130 and 190 Imp gal. The 100 Imp gal came with the Hawk originally, and this was later 'stretched' to 130 Imp gal, while the 190 Imp gal tank is a shortened variant of the 230 Imp gal Hunter tank. As mentioned earlier, the

Above:
In this trial outing during 1978 G-HAWK was loaded with four LAU51 rocket pods.

Right:
Some of the many Hawk external payload options.

Hawk with two 190 Imp gal tanks becomes a reasonably long-range aircraft. Its ferry range in this configuration is 2,200nm, and carrying two Sidewinder air-to-air missiles it has a loiter capability at 30,000ft 100 miles from base of around four hours, so that combat air patrol becomes a very practical propostion.

Sidewinders can be carried on both inboard and outboard stations, and at the time of writing the manufacturer was looking at twin Sidewinders on the outboard station, and was about to clear the Matra Magique for use on the Hawk. A whole range of other missiles was being considered for the aircraft, and a possible option for the future is the carrying of Sidewinders or fuel tanks on wing-tip stations. Royal Air Force Hawks were fitted with three pylon stations, one under each wing, and one beneath the fuselage, for the training role, but a Ministry of Defence decision was taken in the early 1980s to make them adaptable to a war role, mainly for airfield defence. This entailed adapting the wiring to the underwing rails so that each aircraft could carry two Sidewinders. Half the RAF's Mk 1 aircraft were to be adapted, a total of 88, plus the aircraft flown by the Red Arrows, and this work was being carried out by British Aerospace, at Dunsfold, at the rate of 25 aircraft a year after which the modified aircraft are designated Mk 1As. Hawk can also carry a Vinten reconnaissance pod and various devices for target towing. All in all this aircraft, which officially began life with no more pretentions than a fairly simple trainer, has turned into an aeronautical wolf in sheep's clothing. A great deal of the credit for this must go to the design staff at Kingston, which kept this objective firmly in mind.

This capability to be more than just a trainer made the Hawk attractive to the export market, and it was not long before the Mk 50 was being developed to tap overseas sales, to be followed by the Mk 60. Weights went up dramatically, and a tail parachute was fitted. This was an adapted Hunter 'chute on the Mk 50, but on the Mk 60 it had grown to 8ft 8in

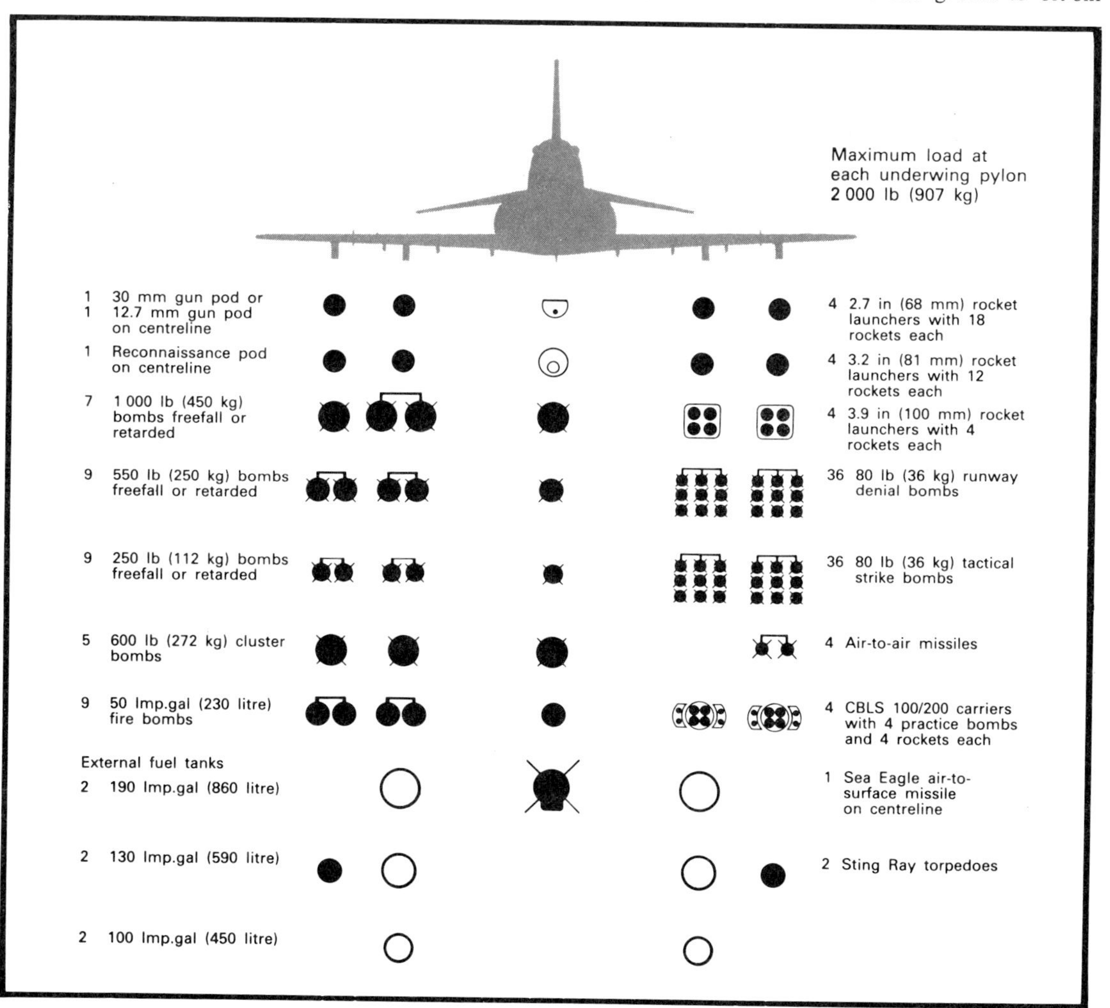

diameter and was fitted as standard. Deployed, it reduces the landing run by 20%. Whereas the RAF Mk 1s operate at 5.7tonne, the export version weighs in at 7.6tonne, and this will go up to 8.6tonne, and even 9.1tonne with some extra thrust from the engine.

The Mk 50 was fitted with the Adour Mk 851 in place of the Mk 151 on the RAF aircraft, the main changes being increased acceleration times, a better engine control amplifier, and improved anti-icing and turbine blade life. The number of pylons was increased from the three on the Mk 1 to five, with the addition of two further wing mountings, and the inboard pylons were cleared to accept 100 Imp gal drop tanks, complete with fuel gauging — which increased the ferry range from 1,335nm to 1,736nm. A fuel-flow meter was fitted, giving more efficient sortie planning and monitoring. A five-station weapon-control system was installed, giving full provision for twin-store carriers on the wing stations. Each pylon was cleared to carry up to 1,135lb under 8G.

Changes to the ejector seats were made at this time, with a smaller headbox fitted to increase the rearward view from both cockpits, and forward vision from the aft cockpit. The need to set the weight of the pilot into the ejector seat was deleted. Some of these changes were later adopted by the RAF. Mk 50s were also given considerable improvements to the avionics and electrics systems, with a

Top:
Hawker Siddeley technicians in practice loading of rocket pods during 1975.

Above:
Matra 116 rocket pods are mated with Hawk outboard pylon in trials in 1976.

Right:
Trial fit of 1,000lb bombs on the pylons of XX161 during 1975.

fully-aerobatic twin gyro attitude and heading reference system, an angle of attack indicator, and, to customer requirements, UHF, VHF, TACAN, VOR, ADF, ILS, and IFF. The shape of the aircraft's tailcone was revised to give improved directional stability at high speed, while weapon-aiming precision was enhanced through alterations to the gearing of longitudinal and lateral controls. Other changes from the Mk 1 included wire-wound oxygen bottles, and a larger-capacity nose equipment bay. This was the version which British Aerospace sold to Finland, where it is known as the Mk 51, the Kenyans (Mk 52) and the Indonesians (Mk 53).

The Mk 60 represented a bigger leap forward, with uprated engine, and aerodynamic improvements to the wing which uprated the aircraft's performance take-off, and also its handling in combat. Rolls-Royce produced the Mk 861 version of the Adour as a private venture, increasing the static thrust at sea level ISA to 5,700lb, a matter of 8%, and by 20% at combat speeds at sea level. Maximum level speed went up from 535kt to 560kt, but the new version of the engine remained completely interchangeable with the Mks 151/851.

Provision was made on the Mk 60 for either 130 Imp gal or 190 Imp gal drop tanks, the latter giving the aircraft a ferry range of 2,176nm. The Mk 60 Hawk was approved for four Sidewinder missiles, two on each outboard pylon, with the pylon stations each cleared to carry 2,000lb. Wheels and tyres were improved to cope with the aircraft's increased weight up to 18,405lb on take-off. The Hawk wing was improved with four-position flaps, and several detailed airflow developments, although the basic shape of the wing was not altered. Changes to the leading-edge stall devices were introduced, as was a new flap angle for take-off. As a result the Mk 60 Hawk has $16\frac{1}{2}$% extra lift under take-off conditions, with the take-off run reduced by 15%. Landing run is reduced by 4%. Other changes included further leg room for the pilots, and the incorporation of longitudinal and lateral trim in the top of the control column.

Some of these improvements in the Mk 60 can be offered to customers which have bought the Mk 50 as retrofits, including twin store carriers, bigger tanks and the wing dressing. At the time of writing, the Mk 60 version had been sold to Zimbabwe (Mk 60), Dubai (Mk 61), Abu Dhabi (Mk 63), and Kuwait (Mk 64). A sale to Venezuela went into cold storage as a result of the Falklands war between Britain and Argentina.

Extending the Hawk family concept still further, British Aerospace developed the Series 100 as an advanced attack variant with a complete change of cockpit instrumentation centred around a nav/attack

Above:
XX158 was involved in private-venture trials during 1977 designed to explore the limits of the Hawk's tolerance of aerodynamically 'dirty' stores.

Below:
Hawk Series 100 equipment.

system based on head-up display (HUD) and inertial navigation system (INS). This was a BAe private venture, with Smiths Industries contributing the development cost of the HUD. All of the advanced avionics and electronics on the Mk 100 are plugged into the MIL-SPEC 1553 digital databus system, and a full-colour, high-brightness, multi-purpose cathode ray tube (CRT) display is fitted.

The Mk 100's systems are optimised for close air support and ground-attack missions, using both conventional and guided air-to-ground weapons. The aircraft also has a full self-defence capability, enhanced by an electronic warfare system, and the ability to carry a wide range of weapons at high speed and low level over a considerable radius of action. The manufacturer claims that it has inherent survivability because of its high attack speeds, its low radar cross-section, and its low infra-red signature.

The INS unit in the Mk 100 is adapted from that in the F-16. The HUD/weapon-aiming computer, developed by Smiths, is new generation equipment, as is a high-accuracy data sensor package. The system is integrated with a view to minimising pilot workload, with all time-critical controls located as part of the HOTAS (hands on throttle and stick) system. The multi-purpose CRT display (MPD), which replaces the conventional attitude and horizontal situation indicators, is also fully integrated into the attack system, and has the potential to display or control any parameter within the system

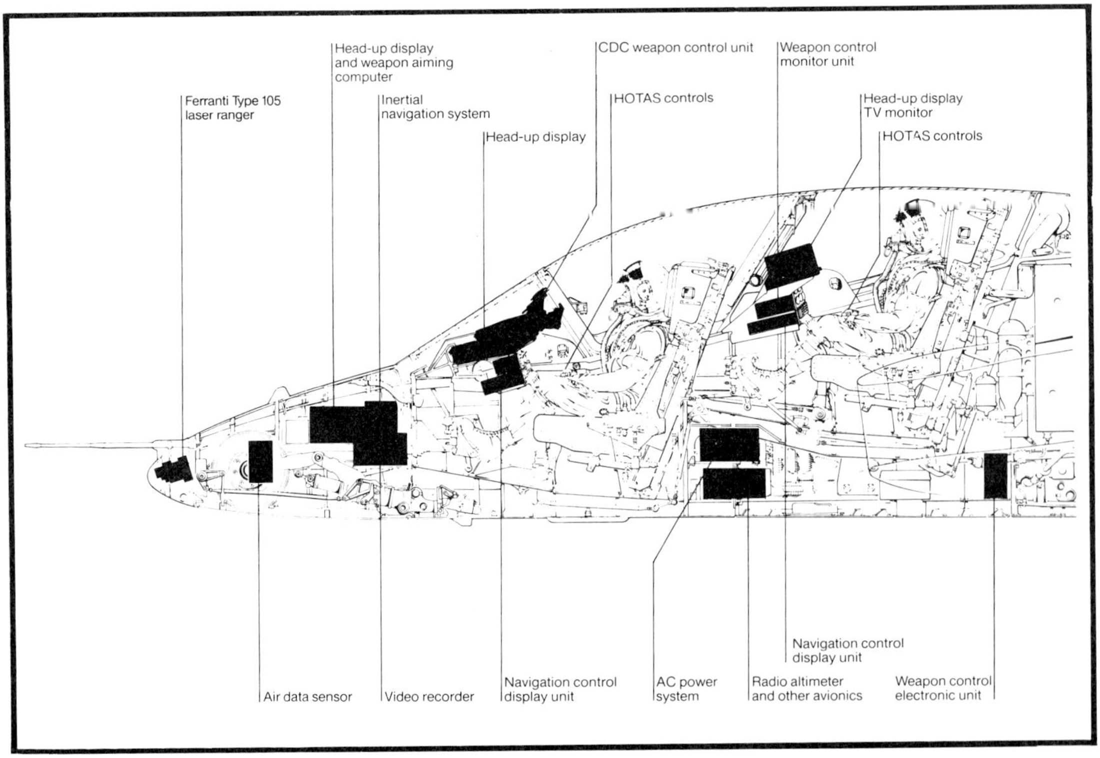

— a unique feature of Hawk 100. The aircraft is also fitted with an on-board passive radar warning receiver, driving a priority threat warning display, and automatically initiating a chaff and flare dispenser unit. The Mk 100 is also capable of carrying a self-powered electronic countermeasure (ECM) pod.

The concept of turning the two-seat Hawk into a single-seat aircraft emerged almost as soon as the basic aircraft went on to the drawing board at Kingston, and the first artist's impressions were around at that factory in the early 1970s. Three factors encouraged HSA's successor, British Aerospace, to pursue the idea as a private venture — the Hawk's performance, its load-carrying capability, and the emergence, during the 1970s, of miniaturised cockpit electronics which would fit comfortably into the small Hawk airframe, and which looked set fair to alter an entire industry's thinking on what the optimum size of the 'fighter' aircraft of the future ought to be. By the early 1980s BAe was offering the single-seat Hawk, coded the Series 200, to potential purchasers around the world, and was planning a prototype. The Hawk 200 was seen not as an interceptor, but as a fast reconnaissance aircraft — with cameras built into the nose — as a night ground-attack and reconnaissance aircraft — using infra-red — and, equipped with long-range radar, as a barrier air defence aircraft with genuine over-water capability, or as a maritime aircraft with anti-ship and anti-submarine missiles. A wide range of weapons could be carried.

British Aerospace felt that in the Hawk it had a basis for a light multi-role aircraft, and that removal of one pilot, his cockpit, systems, and ejector seat, occupying up to 50cu ft in volume, would leave ample room for a wide variety of warlike equipment and stores. Existing structure and systems aft of the rear cockpit bulkhead were retained in the 200 design, but ahead of that point a completely new forward fuselage was designed. The mass and volume previously required to accommodate the student thus became available for a built-in gun installation and 300 rounds of ammunition. Two guns, rather than the single gun carried externally on the centreline pylon, with 100 rounds of ammunition, were proposed, an obvious added advantage in case of jamming in action. This, in turn, freed the centreline pylon to carry a wide selection of stores, including Sea Eagle, additional external fuel, bombs, countermeasure equipment, or reconnaissance pods.

29

And there was still space left in the nose to fit advanced sensing systems, such as a radar with a 24in dish. The equipment options offered on the 200 aircraft are, in fact, very wide. They range from the fit used in the Mk 60 series, with a beacon-based navigation system and a conventional gunsight, giving a day VMC operational capability, through a fit incorporating FLIR and laser to give a night VMC role, to a full, advanced avionics suite with head-up display, inertial navigation, radar, multi-purpose cathode ray tube display and hands on throttle and stick system to provide a long-range, all weather, missile launching capability.

The single-seat Hawk reversed the trend in world aerospace towards bigger, heavier and more complex

Above:
Plans to turn the Hawk into a single-seater existed as early as 1976, as this artist's impression of that time shows. Main external difference between this model and today's 200 series single-seater is that the single cannon carried on the centreline has been replaced by twin guns stowed internally.

fighter aircraft, which had resulted in a proliferation of prohibitively-expensive machines weighing anything up to 30tonne apiece. Air forces, worried by high fuel prices, mounting maintenance costs and reduced annual budgets, were attracted by the significant reduction in vehicle size, and therefore spending, represented by the Hawk 200, and by the fact that this was not something untried and new, but

Above:
1983 artist's impression of the proposed series 200 single-seat version of the Hawk. Port for the left-hand internal gun can be seen aft of the laser chin fairing. This is the night ground attack variant of the 200.

Hawk 200 basic data

Overall length: 36ft 3in
Span: 30ft 10in
Height: 13ft 2in
Wing area: 179.64sq ft
Thickness/chord ratio (root): 10.9%
Thickness/chord ratio (tip): 9%
Leading edge sweep: 26°
Quarter chord sweep: 21.5°
Empty weight: 9,150lb
Max take-off weight: 20,062lb
Internal fuel: 3,000lb (375 Imp gal)
External fuel: 3,040lb (380 Imp gal)
Stressing limits, full internal load: +8G, −4G
Stressing limits, 3,000lb warload plus 60% internal fuel: +8G, −4G
Max dive speed: Mach 1.2
Max level speed: 560kt
Max altitude: 50,000ft
Max warload: 6,800lb

Data is for beginning of 1984; BAe has emphasised that the specification could change at any time.

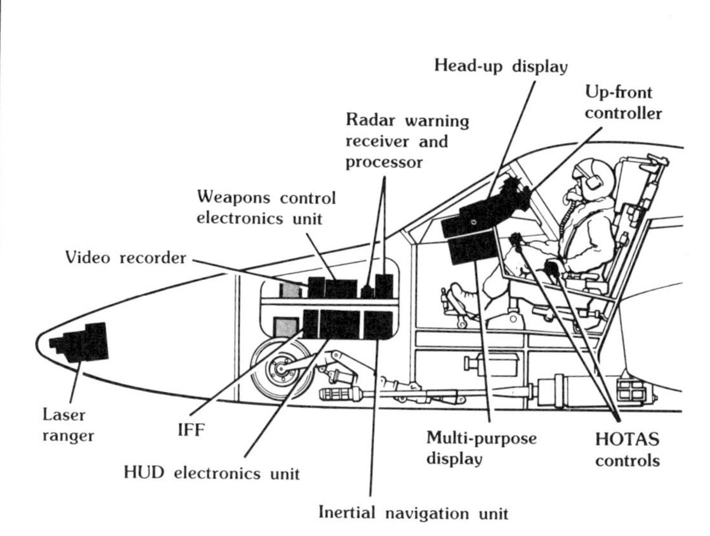

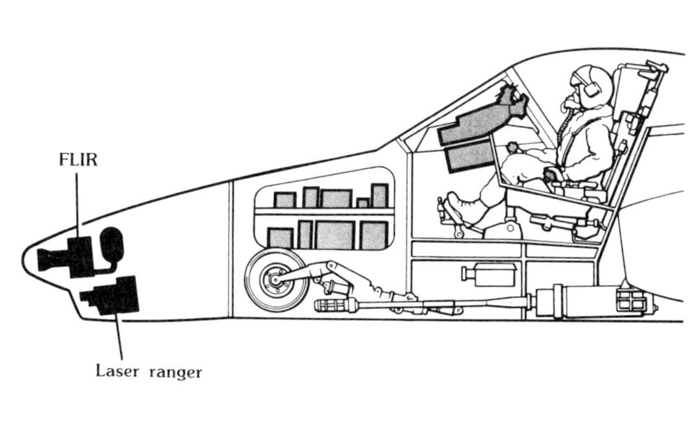

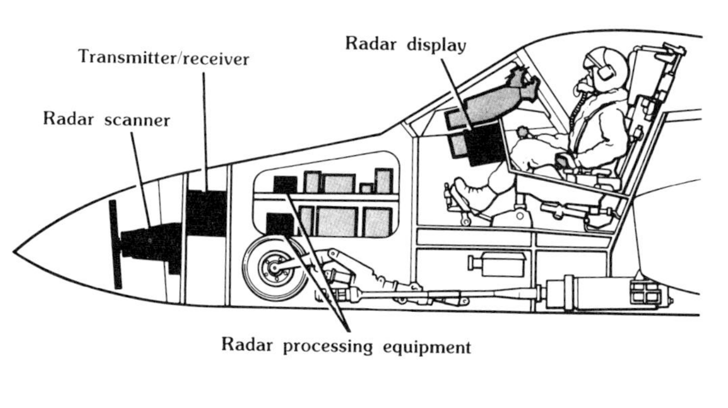

Left:

British Aerospace promoted the Series 200 single-seat Hawk in three main equipment configurations for day, night and all-weather operations.

Left:

(i) DAY

The aircraft can be fitted with a conventional gyro-stabilised attack sight and attitude heading reference system (AHRS), with navigation using a variety of radio aids. Navigation and weapon aiming capabilities are considerably improved by fitting an inertial navigation system (INS), allied to a head-up display (HUD) and powerful weapon aiming computer (WAC). The INS acts as the central reference platform, integrated with the aircraft's nav/attack system via a databus, and forms the basis of Hawk 200's high technology precision navigation and attack systems. The optional laser provides precise target slant range data to the WAC enabling it to perform the continuous trigonometric solutions associated with the ballistic characteristics of each selected weapon.

Left:

(ii) NIGHT

The forward looking infra-red (FLIR) equipment converts very low ambient light conditions to almost daylight standards, allowing Hawk 200 to carry out precision ground attacks and tactical reconnaissance by day and night.

Left:

(iii) ALL-WEATHER

An advanced multi-mode radar adds all-weather target acquisition and navigational fixing capabilities. As well as ground attack operations, the radar allows Hawk 200 to carry out long-range anti-shipping strikes using such weapons as the Sea Eagle missile. Medium range air-to-air missiles such as Sky Flash 90 can also be employed.

a member of an aircraft family which had shown its paces, and not been found wanting, over a decade. Miniaturisation of avionics during the period that Hawk had been developing through its trainer phase into a strike aircraft had meant not only that more equipment could be packed into a small space, but that that equipment could be managed by a single crew member, instead of by two, and that its power requirements could be packed into the Hawk fuselage. The advent of long-range 'smart' weapons during that same period, compatible with the Hawk's carrying capacity, made it feasible to contemplate a variant of this small aircraft with operational capabilities normally associated with machines two or even three times the weight of the Hawk. It was also not lost on potential purchasers of the single-seater, or indeed on those which opted for any of the other marks of Hawk, that with so many versions in operation in both Britain and abroad, it is guaranteed that the Hawk will continue well into the 21st century, and that further evolutions of the basic aircraft are still possible, given the inherent 'stretchability' of airframe and engine.

In external appearance the single-seat Hawk is readily identifiable by its smaller canopy and its larger nose, and this in turn could have three alternative shapes, depending on equipment options. For daylight operations the Series 200 could be equipped with a conventional gyro-stabilised attack sight and attitude heading reference system, its navigation

utilising a range of radio aids. The inertial navigation system could be linked to a head-up display and a weapon-aiming computer, with the INS acting as a central reference platform, integrated via a databus with the navigation/attack system, and forming the foundation of the aircraft's high-tech, precision navigation and attack systems. For night operations, forward-looking infra-red equipment carried in the nose would convert conditions of extremely-low ambient light conditions to approaching daylight

Below:
An RAF Valley trainer Hawk stands on its tail above the overcast. The pyramid and palm tree markings on its tail fin commemorate the original location of No 4 FTS in Egypt.

standards. This, allied to a laser ranger, would enable Hawk to carry out precision ground attacks and tactical reconnaissance missions. In its all-weather mode, the Hawk 200 would be fitted with an advanced multi-mode radar to give it target acquisition under poor conditions, plus precise navigational fixing capability. The radar would also enable the aircraft to carry out long-range anti-shipping strikes carrying Sea Eagle, while medium range air-to-air missiles such as Sky Flash 90 could also be employed.

British Aerospace promoted the Hawk 200 single-seat on a number of other platforms, as well as that of its wide range of avionic systems. It was pointed out to prospective purchasers that with its small size and high speed at low level, together with its very low radar and infra-red signature, it is extremely difficult to detect. Its warload is large and varied, and the aircraft's handling and flying qualities, and manoeuvring limits, remain virtually unimpaired even when carrying an array of large and heavy stores. With a warload of 3,000lb, and 60% of fuel remaining in typical overhead battlefield conditions, the full combat load factor of 8G remains available, and with store loads in excess of this weight the permitted load factor is still 5.5G. A capacity of 2,000lb is available at each of the four underwing pylons.

The low fuel consumption of the Adour would enable the Hawk 200, equipped with missiles, to remain on patrol, unrefuelled, for four hours at 100nm from its base — a capability which would require many more individual patrol sorties by most other aircraft. It was also claimed by BAe that the single-seat Hawk would have superior persistence in combat, its efficient wing and low fuel flows at maximum power giving it the ability to outperform and outlast the opposition at low and medium altitudes.

Ferry range, equipped with two 190 Imp gal external tanks is 2,200nm without refuelling. The Hawk is also being promoted on grounds of low first and operating costs and, for operators of two-seat Hawks, reduced experience, spares and ground-servicing equipment costs. The aircraft needs only minimum manpower on the ground. Each aircraft requires only four technicians to support it for organisational, intermediate and depot-level maintenance, representing a significant reduction in manpower when compared with heavier, larger and more-costly aircraft of similar capability. Marginal increases in maintenance manpower will depend on the particular avionic and sensor options chosen.

Powerplant for the Hawk 200 is the Mk 861 Adour with a maximum static thrust at sea level of 5,700lb. This has 11 small and easily-handled modules, interchangeable between engines, and independently replaceable without the need to rebalance rotating assemblies, resulting in a 30% reduction of spares. The engine is mounted on the airframe on three attachment points in the same way as on the earlier Hawk variants, and has a simple dropout installation which enables engine changes to be carried out in under two hours.

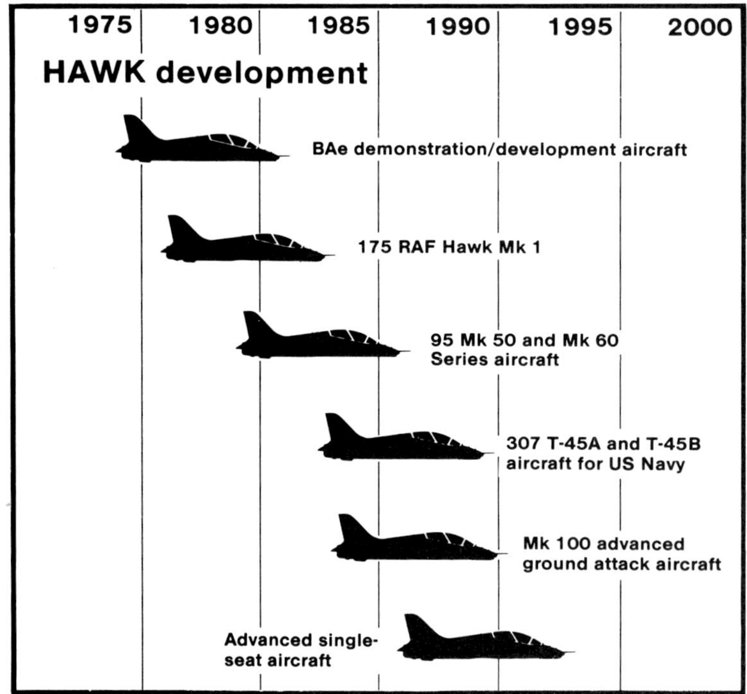

Right:
The 'scratch' team of Hawks for the 1976 Farnborough displays. The team is led by Duncan Simpson in XX156 carrying Sidewinders and drop tanks, the first time Hawk had been demonstrated in public carrying hardware), followed by G-HAWK, in desert camouflage.
BAe via Duncan Simpson

Below:
A Brawdy Hawk produces an impressive burst of flame as
it fires Matra 155 rocket pods.

Bottom:
Eight Brawdy Hawks line up on a rainswept hard standing.

Top:
Inverted, and in perfect formation over the English countryside, the Red Arrows go through a practice session in 1980. Belly tanks holding the oil and dye for the smoke trails can be seen clearly.

Above:
A Brawdy Hawk awaits servicing on the flight line.

4 First Flight

First flight of the first Hawk, XX154, took place at the Hawker Siddeley Aviation airfield at Dunsfold, Surrey on 21 August 1974, in the early evening with Duncan Simpson, Chief Test Pilot of the Kingston division of HSA, at the controls. According to the pilot's notes the all-up weight of the aircraft, which was painted in the red and white livery that it would wear when it eventually went to the RAF, was 4,946kg, and its internal tanks were fully loaded with 1,250kg of fuel. The wind was very light — less than 5kt — the runway was dry, and there was 15km-plus visibility, with 4-6/8 cloud at 3-5,000ft and the top of the haze layer at 5,000ft. At the end of the runway the aircraft was held on the brakes while the engine was accelerated to 90% high-pressure spool revolutions per minute (rpm). Then the brakes were released, and the engine accelerated to full power. Even with full fuel, the acceleration was found to be lively, and after an initial touch of brake to keep straight, the rudder soon became effective. The nose lifted off the runway, as anticipated, at 105kt indicated air speed (IAS).

XX154 became airborne for the first time at 120kt, flying smoothly off the ground. The notes recall that the quietness and smoothness of the aircraft were most impressive, even with the undercarriage extended. Cabin conditioning was the loudest noise, and the powerful jets of air from the cockpit sides became an embarrassment, making writing on the knee pad difficult, with the paper being blown up by the blast (this was later cured by a redistribution of the cabin air). Level flight was

temporarily held at 2,000ft, and 150kt maintained at 92%rpm, until cleared to climb to 5,000ft. With 95%rpm set, 170kt IAS gave a comfortable climb to that altitude. Some cloud interfered momentarily with the retraction of the undercarriage, since the sequence had to be recorded on film, but visual conditions were obtained after easing up to 6,000ft (the maiden flight was being filmed from two chase aircraft, a two-seat Hunter flown by Andy Jones, and the HSA Harrier demonstrator G-VTOL flown by John Farley). Speed was reduced to 150kt and

stabilised conditions established before the undercarriage was selected up. Retraction appeared to by symmetrical, with slight transient trim nose-up; time to retract was approximately nine seconds. Flaps were raised at 170kt, causing negligible trim change over a period of eight seconds. Speed was then increased to 250kt, then decreased for preliminary airbrake investigation. Light nose-down transient trim change occurred over the first second of a 1½sec extension, although the resultant trim change was negligible.

A straight climb was then made to 20,000ft at 90%rpm and at 250kt, and during the climb a check was made on all the aircraft systems and oxygen. At 20,000ft, the cockpit instruments indicated oxygen ⅞ full and fuel state 1,000kg. At 170kt IAS, mid-flap was lowered, and at 150kt, with tailplane trimmed to -2°, the undercarriage was lowered, taking six seconds to lock down. Handling on the approach to the stall was satisfactory, with no indication of pre-stall buffet down to 112kt IAS, and with the incidence gauge showing 11°, the agreed maximum for first flight. The flaps were then lowered fully at 130kt and the speed reduced to 105kt IAS. The fuel

G-HAWK
HAWK

Above:
Still in imitation USN training livery during 1984, the company demonstrator is seen here fitted with a pair of Matra Magique missiles on the outboard stations.

Below:
The second Mk 53 for Indonesia carries production drop tanks without fins and rear cones. The gun pod has its gun removed and nose blanked off ready for ferrying.

state was then 930kg. Time was now running short due to the light conditions below cloud, and it was felt that sufficient information had been obtained to land with full flap, especially with the almost calm conditions prevailing at base.

An initial descent was then made to 10,000ft, where some gentle turning manoeuvres were made at 250kt IAS. During the further descent from 10,000ft, IAS was increased to 310kt, with 840kg fuel remaining.

The pilot's notes indicate that on entering the circuit speed was decreased to 170kt on a wide downwind position, where mid-flap was extended. Speed was further decreased to 150kt, when the undercarriage was lowered. Rpm was maintained to about 80%rpm to give a gradual decrease of IAS to 130kt, half way round the final approach. Full flap was lowered at about two miles, and speed reduced to 120kt, with 80% fan rpm, and -3° tailplane. It was immediately apparent that the effect of full flap had caused a reduction in descent rate, and it needed some 10% reduction in rpm and a conscious effort to put the nose down to regain and maintain an approximate 3° flight path to the runway. The speed was reduced gradually to 110kt at a half mile — only the ailerons felt as if they might be less than desirably effective if the conditions had been otherwise than calm. The mainwheels touched lightly at about 95kt, and the nose was held up for about three seconds. As had been found on the high-speed taxi run before first light, the nose seemed to lower on to the runway for ever, and there was little evidence that the nosewheel had touched. Light to moderate braking brought the aircraft to rest in about half the runway length. The Hawk was then taxied back along the runway and into dispersal, when there was 740kg fuel remaining.

First flight on that summer's evening of 1974 was, in fact, the culmination for Duncan Simpson of four years meticulous preparation from the time when he succeeded Hugh Merewether as Chief Pilot in 1970. He was joined in this preparation by Andy Jones, as Project Pilot, and Jim Hawkins, as Second Project Pilot. Both had joined Hawker Siddeley Aviation from the Fighter Test Squadron at Boscombe Down. They brought with them a wealth of experience to the

Left:
Duncan Simpson, Chief Test Pilot, Kingston Division of HSA (left), and Andy Jones, Hawk Project Pilot, stand before the red-and-white painted first Hawk, XX154, after roll-out. In the background is one of the aircraft the Hawk was to replace in the training role, the two-seat Hunter.
BAe via Duncan Simpson

Above right:
XX154 in the engine running pen at Dunsfold prior to first taxi runs, August 1974. The Hunter exhaust system was adapted to accommodate the new aircraft. Can on the probe provides protection on the ground for the delicate yaw and angle of attack vanes.

Right:
The towbar is disconnected from the tractor as XX154 arrives on the hard standing at Dunsfold for the first time before beginning taxi runs.

Below:
BAe's two demonstrators, G-HAWK, flown by J. S. Hawkins, and Harrier G-VTOL, flown by H. E. Frick, return in formation from the Paris air show in 1979.

Bottom:
During 1983 Hawk XX258 was used as a Sea Eagle anti-ship missile trials aircraft. Here 258 is seen carrying the missile on its centreline pylon; tests were also made with additional combinations of drop tanks and Sidewinder AAMs on the wing pylons.

Above:
XX205, on loan from RAF Brawdy to the manufacturer for the 1978 Farnborough air show, poses in front of the Seven Sisters.

Below:
XX261 from RAF Brawdy turns on to finals with gear and flaps down.

Hawk project, since both were Royal Air Force test pilots with flying instructor categories. They also had extensive operational and weapons experience, which was also essential to the development of this new and advanced trainer aircraft, with its ground-attack and all-round weapons capability.

This pilot team liaised closely with the design staff at HSA Kingston and at regular progress meetings in London with the Procurement Executive of the Ministry of Defence, on all matters of detail which would affect the aircraft's eventual performance. Their inputs helped to determine the layout and choice of equipment and the placing of instruments in the cockpit of the wood and metal mock-up which HSA built in the Kingston factory.

Endless trouble was taken to ensure that both instructor and student should have the best possible view through the hood and the windshield, and a cockpit mock-up in which pilots and design staff could sit was placed on the back of an elderly lorry and run up and down the Dunsfold runway. Martin Baker was persuaded to modify the headbox of its ejector seat destined for the front cockpit of the Hawk so that the instructor in the rear seat would have increased vision on either side.

The team was aided in this vital preliminary work by the fact that aviation technology was moving fast at the beginning of the 1970s, with industrial capabilities of making large, one-piece canopies with the correct optics showing big advances, and with miniaturisation and computers making quantum jumps. Although a lot of Gnat and Hunter experience went into the Hawk, the pilot team was determined that the cockpits on the new aircraft should be well laid out with the sort of modern instruments and equipment which the students would

Left:
First flight! Duncan Simpson up, the first Hawk gets off the ground for the first time, from Dunsfold, in the early evening of 21 August 1974.

Top:
The clean lines of the new Hawker 'baby' were immediately apparent as soon as Duncan Simpson got the gear up on the maiden outing. XX154 is flying above the overcast, and the shadows on the fuselage indicate how late in the day it was.

Above:
Slowing down, with gear extended and mid flap, on the maiden outing, and with the Hunter chase aircraft in close attendance.

Above:
The G-HAWK demonstrator in a vertical dive during trials of a new ADF aerial in the fin root.

Above:
Safely down. Duncan Simpson lands back at Dunsfold after a successful first flight in XX154, the first Hawk. Picture was taken from the HSA Harrier demonstrator G-VTOL, which had acted as chase 'plane along with the Hunter. The Harrier was flown by John Farley, who followed Duncan down the runway, and landed close by.

find when they progressed to their eventual front-line operational aircraft types. Right from the start the aircraft which were to be used in the test programme were well-equipped with TACAN, multi-channel UHF and VHF radios, and an instrument landing system.

This equipment paid dividends during the development flying programme because, unlike many earlier prototype aircraft, which had been kitted out with a bare minimum of equipment, the Hawks were able to fly test sorties of up to $2\frac{1}{2}$ hours, which frequently covered three or four different test programmes, even if the weather was bad. This accelerated flight-test programme was assisted by a computer system at Dunsfold on which the results of each flight could be analysed quickly. Inevitably there had to be compromises between what would have been ideal and what the budget, very carefully controlled in the case of the Hawk, would stand.

Finally the first aircraft took shape at Kingston and was then shipped by road to Dunsfold where the wings and fuselage, already complete with all the systems, were mated. Roll-out behind a tractor was carried out without ceremony early in August 1974, and for the first time the complete shape of the sleek new aircraft was revealed to the public eye, the main change since original design being a lowering of the engine intake position from high up on the fuselage to low down, after wind tunnel tests had shown that the latter was more efficient.

Two weeks of engine runs followed, during which the cabin-conditioning and other engine-powered systems were checked, and the first two taxi runs on the Dunsfold runway took place on 20 August —

during which a stiffness in the nosewheel castoring manifested itself. At the end of the second run, just as a precaution, the Hawk was offered up to the overrun barrier at the end of the runway, from which it could be seen that the barrier would be adequate to stop the aircraft in an emergency, and that the canopy would not be damaged. Two further taxi runs were made on 21 August, and as with the two the previous day, Duncan Simpson was at the controls. On the first run on the 21st, the ram-air turbine functioning was checked and the tail parachute (fitted against the possibility of deep stalling, rather than for the purpose of runway deceleration) streamed at 90kt, and jettisoned at 30kt. A maximum speed of 90kt on this run had been agreed, and at this speed the nose rose abruptly off the runway. The nose-up pitch was checked, the throttle closed, and tail parachute selected immediately. The incident confirmed the need for a second run to look at nosewheel off, and control in pitch with a tailplane setting of zero, instead of -2°, before committing the aircraft to first take-off.

In the second fast taxi run zero trim was selected with mid-flap — the chosen condition for first take-off. The aircraft was accelerated, and the nosewheel

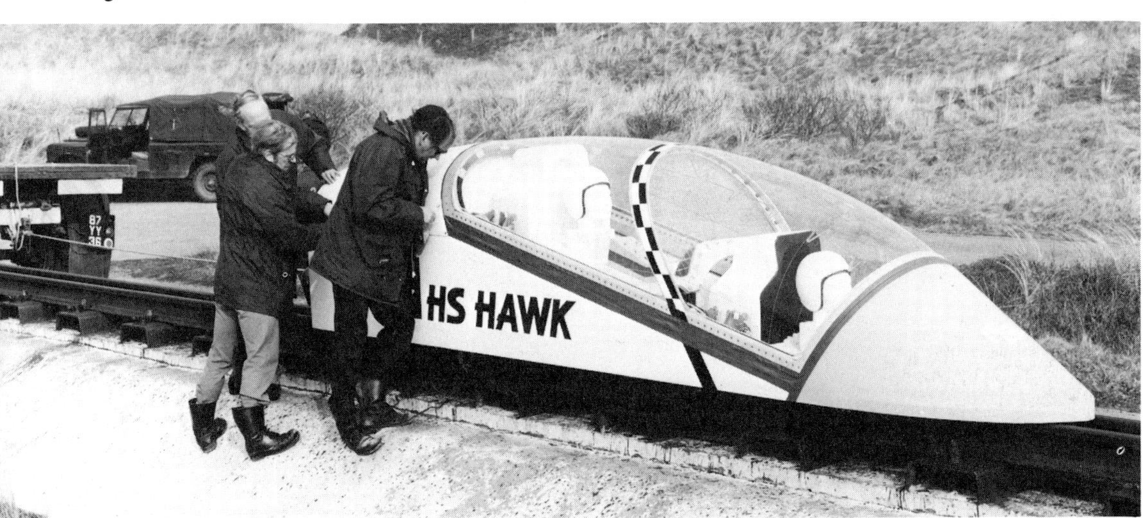

raised with gentle back pressure on the control column at about 95kt IAS. The aircraft attitude was checked with the nosewheel off the ground at an estimated 4ft. After a brief assessment the throttle was closed and the nose lowered — 'it seemed to drop for ever', say the pilot's notes — on to the runway. The point was made that it is usual in a nosewheel-type aircraft that contact with the runway is barely perceptible, even with considerable terminal velocity. The forward view with the nose up was good, and this only tended to accentuate the superb forward vision when the nose dropped. At that point it was felt that sufficient experience had been gained to proceed with confidence with the first flight.

That occasion took place later that same day, and less than 24 hours after the first taxi run. Safety was obviously paramount, but there was urgency from two points of view — the weather forecast for 22 August was not particularly favourable (it in fact turned out to be a fine day) and the 1974 Farnborough air show, at which it was planned to display the paces of the new aircraft before the public for the first time, was just under a fortnight away. The final arbiter was to be the light conditions and general weather on the evening of the 21st, but soon after 7pm — XX154 had been refuelled and made ready after its second taxi run, its tail parachute repacked and rearmed — conditions remained good, and the decision was made to go. By the time the aircraft returned to Dunsfold the light was starting to fail and navigation lights were switched on for the approach and landing. By the time Duncan Simpson had completed his checks after landing and had taxied back to dispersal, a further 10 minutes had passed and it was 8.30pm. In typical HSA tradition, the small reception committee was outwardly matter-of-fact over the important event which had just occurred in the company's history, but after the pilot had climbed out of the front cockpit there was an instant debriefing, followed later by a celebratory drink in the Dunsfold mess.

Second flight took place without any loss of time the following morning, 22 August, again with Duncan Simpson up, and on the third flight, later that same day, Andy Jones was in charge. Among the features of the second sortie were a shallow dive to Mach 0.8, reduction of speed to 96kt with no pre-stall buffet, selection of the airbrake during a descent to 10,000ft at 250kt, and the pulling of 3G and then 4G at 380kt IAS. No 2 hydraulic system was deliberately failed at 200kt, causing the ram-air turbine to extend, the motor of which was immediately apparent as it wound up, giving a distinct though unobtrusive vibration through the airframe. The No 2 system was then reselected and the ram-air turbine reset. A second failure was selected to enable the chase aircraft to photograph the ram-air turbine's extension and retraction. On the fourth flight, with Duncan Simpson flying, the Hawk was inverted three times over Boscombe Down. After the third of these the aircraft was rolled out after six seconds. Almost full aileron was used, and it was soon apparent that the ailerons had jammed in the fully-deflected position. Considerable force was necessary with both hands to return the ailerons to

Below:
Hawks began to appear in the test programme carrying stores during 1975. This aircraft, probably XX158, has two CBLS (carrier bomb light store) under the wings. The pitot boom is well-instrumented.

Left:
**Maintainability of the Adour engine
in the Hawk was successfully
demonstrated as part of the MoD
contract during 1975.**

Below:
**Unusual rear-end view of one of the
early Hawks taken during 1975 at
Dunsfold, probably during
maintainability trials.**

Above:
HSA test pilot Jim Hawkins took the XX156 to Luqa, Malta during 1975 for warm-weather trials.

neutral. Following the control jam, a descent was made with minimum aileron movement, lateral control being maintained with rudder. The circuit and landing were uneventful, the pilot's notes record laconically.

The early test programme continued to proceed speedily (the cause of the obstruction having been established), and on its ninth flight the Hawk was ferried by Duncan Simpson to the Farnborough show, where he demonstrated it in the flying display each day, often in appalling weather with powerful crosswinds. HSA staff had worked night and day to have the aircraft ready for Farnborough, and by that time it had spent about 10 hours in the air. On its arrival at the show, the new aircraft excited considerable attention among aviation people gathered there, and not least among the RAF Red Arrows aerobatic team, which had brought in its Gnats

ready for the show. Two of the team ran straight across to the Hawk when it parked and were quickly crawling all over it, with the query, 'When are we going to be allowed to get our hands on it?' In fact, the team switched to Hawks $4\frac{1}{2}$ years later, and gave its first performance with them at the 1980 Farnborough show, six years to the day after that first landing there of Hawk number one, XX154.

As the aircraft was still in the early stages of its development programme, manoeuvres in the 1974 air show flying display were naturally limited, but sufficient was done with it to prove that here was a new trainer aircraft with out-of-the-ordinary performance and handling qualities. XX154 was free from unserviceability right through the show, and each day its performance included a very tight turn after take-off, a slow barrel roll starting and finishing at 200ft, tight turns and reversals, and a Derry turn — an inverted reverse — before landing to the plaudits of the crowd. As one aviation journal reported, 'The Hawk display was amongst the smoothest in the show, with never a jerky movement.'

XX154 appeared at Farnborough not with the comprehensive flight-test instrumentation that had been planned, but with a simple and temporary flight recording system, because of the short time between first flight and the opening day of the show. On its return to Dunsfold from Farnborough, installation of the instrumentation was carried out and XX154 flew again, some three months later, on 19 December that year. Two modifications were made to the flying control system as a result of the initial flying — linear gearing in the ailerons control circuit was introduced to give better lateral control, particularly in the approach configuration in gusty conditions, and spring centring of the rudder was added to improve directional characteristics, particularly in partial rolls with the undercarriage down.

Both these alterations proved satisfactory during 10 hours of shakedown flying which followed when XX154 returned to flight status. Assessments were also made during this second phase of flying of handling with the nose undercarriage doors locked up and the leg extended in an attempt to improve directional

Above:

First carriage of Matra 155s was on XX154 during 1975; this picture was taken near Littlehampton, on the English south coast, XX154, the original Hawk, acts as chase aircraft for experiments with pilotless drones at RAE Llanbedr, Wales, among other duties.

stability in the landing pattern — which did not prove significant — and of limited stalling with the aircraft 'clean', and in the approach configuration. These tests were made with the original inboard wing fence fitted, and the stalling speeds matched predicted values closely. But wing drop at the stall was too rapid for a trainer, and in any case it was not representative of the modern combat aircraft. The buffet warning before the wing drop was also considered insufficient.

Hot and cold relights of the Adour were obtained at 20,000ft mainly as a confidence check on such action in case of inadvertent extinction in flight, and also to confirm some of the tests which had already been obtained at the Rolls-Royce test facility at

Derby. The anti-spin parachute was streamed three times in the air prior to stalling, and the aircraft was flown at night for an assessment of the night lighting installation. On several occasions during this phase of flying the aircraft was landed back at base in dusk to night conditions. Phase two of the test flying came to an end on 7 January 1975, and XX154 was immediately prepared for the flutter clearance programme. Ground resonance tests on the number two aircraft had been almost completed by this stage.

The initial flutter clearance was up to 400kt IAS and 0.8 indicated Mach number (IMN). Increases in IAS were then given at increments of 50kt to a maximum of 550kt, and at high altitude a 0.02 IMN increase was allowed. It was found that a substantial position error had been present, and the 0.8 IMN which had been achieved was, in fact, 0.85 true. Natural turbulence was relied upon for airframe excitation, and the procedure for clearing a flutter point was to accelerate the aircraft through the newly-cleared speed band, having repeated the speed cleared from the previous flight. When the new speed or Mach number was reached, it was maintained for at least 90 seconds. IAS clearances were normally flown at 3,000ft, and Mach number clearances at 30,000ft. In addition, a dive was carried out at a constant Mach number indicated until the combination of cleared IMN and IAS occurred. Only moderate angles of dive, of between 8° and 10°, were necessary to achieve the specification speeds of 550kt IAS and 0.9° IMN combination. Drag was therefore proving much less than had been predicted.

The Hawk also appeared faster than had been predicted at altitude, and it was flutter-cleared at this stage up to 0.98 IMN in a 30° dive from 40,000ft — estimated at 1.1 true Mach number. Opportunity was also taken during the flutter clearance to assess handling at each speed increment, and small changes were made wherever possible to improve characteristics by applying fixes in the wing. This work consisted of fitting two rows of vortex generators on the top surface to improve handling at high speed, the replacing of the original inboard fence by a larger fence further outboard, and the adding of a leading-edge breaker strip to introduce pre-stall buffet warning.

When the IMN was increased from 0.8 to 0.84, a noticeable deterioration in longitudinal stability occurred, and random pitch changes made the aircraft quite difficult to fly accurately, although at no time did the situation feel precarious, with lateral and directional control remaining good. On progressing to 0.86 IMN, the longitudinal problems evaporated, and with further IMN this improvement was maintained. It had been predicted that vortex generators fitted to the top surface of the wing would improve the longitudinal handling in the 0.82 to 0.84 IMN region, and this in fact proved correct. Two rows of vortex generators were fitted for the initial modification of the wing, but at a later stage the rear row was proved redundant, and was removed.

On increasing IMN to 0.9 (0.96 true Mach number) a rolling moment occurred which could require up to half aileron to counteract. Aileron control remained positive if degraded in this range, even with positive or negative G applied. Subsequent increases in IMN did not involve any further handling abnormalities, and it was evident at this stage

Left:
During 1976 XX154 was loaned back to HSA for private venture trials carrying five 1,000lb bombs. The pilot on this occasion was Mike Snelling.

Below:
Farnborough '76 formation team Hawks line up on the ground. The display was mounted at short notice, but the team arrived over the show within seconds of target time on each of the three days that it flew. *BAe via Duncan Simpson*

that the Hawk would achieve higher Mach numbers more easily, and with significantly better handling, than had been predicted. The aircraft spent some considerable time between 500 and 550kt IAS, and was subjected to extremes of turbulence, where apart from some care being necessary longitudinally, it was pleasant to fly and manoeuvre. It was found that with the clean aircraft a level speed of 530kt IAS could be achieved and maintained.

The Hawk had been stalled in all configurations, from clean aircraft to undercarriage and full flap down, with and without external stores, and after some preliminary stalling with the inboard fences, which were only fitted for early flying on information from wind tunnel tests, it was decided that a start should be made with a completely clean wing. The Hawk wing was designed to be highly efficient, and as such tends to be somewhat unforgiving. Although some very low stalling speeds were obtained, the buffet warning with the clean wing was minimal, and the wing drop with full flap and undercarriage down could reach some 90° per second.

It was therefore decided to provide two 'taming' fixes — both of which had been well tried on other aircraft. These were the wing fence, added outboard, to desensitise the wing drop at the stall, and the leading-edge breaker strip to provide some buffet warning, particularly with flaps extended. With these fixes the clean stall was found to be innocuous, with some 10kt buffet warning before stick hard back in moderate buffet at about 25° incidence, accompanied by subdued lateral wing low effects. Recovery was immediate on releasing the stick forward.

Powerful flaps had made the approach configuration stall more difficult to civilise. Even with wing fences, some rapid wing drop had been experienced without the breaker strip. But with the breaker strip fitted, buffet warning on the stall was introduced over a band of 5kt, and the behaviour was reduced to wing low effects, which could reverse if the stick was held back, with no tendency to depart in roll. As in the clean stall, recovery was immediate in releasing the control column. A traditional wing-tufting method was employed in both high and low

Above:
HSA put its first four Hawks, XX154, XX156, XX157 and XX158, in the air together for a photo call during 1976.

Left:
1976 photo call for the first four Hawks. XX156, nearest the camera, is camouflaged, the other three (from the camera) XX158, XX157 and XX154, were in red and white RAF training finish. Roles were: XX154 primarily handling, XX156 weapons and systems, XX157 primarily systems, and XX158 spinning.

Above right:
In 1977 the number four development aircraft, XX158, was on loan to the manufacturers for Sidewinder carrying trials. In this picture the ram air turbine forward of the fin is deployed, and a non-standard temperature probe fitted on the left side of the nose.

speed investigations. Cameras were mounted on the gunsight platform in the rear cockpit, and the film which was obtained showed clearly both the high Mach number shock wave effect, and the 'untamed' and 'tamed' wing at the stall, with flaps and undercarriage down. The engine performed well throughout the flight envelope during this phase, and handling, performance and reliability were all considered to be highly encouraging.

Phase four of the Hawk development programme began with the first flight of XX157 in April 1975. Although XX154 had achieved a satisfactory standard in handling at the stall, it soon became apparent that subsequent aircraft were not consistent in their behaviour, particularly in the approach configuration with undercarriage and full flap. Lateral effects were variable, and seemed to be sensitive to surface finish on the wing.

On this occasion the aircraft pitched nose down over the vertical to -12° incidence with full back stick, before recovering when the flaps were retracted. Further investigations proved that the tailplane could be deliberately stalled with full flap down and undercarriage up at all altitudes down to 5,000ft provided that suitable, if somewhat harsh, methods were employed in pulling the control column fully aft. This problem was effectively cured by cutting out the outboard section of the flap slot vane. As a further precaution, the tailplane travel

was reduced from -17° to -15°. There was a strong temptation to experiment in cutting down the existing outboard fence, but one move in this direction proved counter-productive. An outboard breaker strip was added, however, and whatever small improvement resulted in the 1G stall, there was an encouraging bonus in the high-speed stall, where an undesirable 'snatching' was removed, and handling at high incidence generally improved. As a result of this work, the Hawk can now be stalled with a high degree of confidence in all configurations.

Aircraft number four, XX158, was used for deliberate mishandling and spinning trials. It was fitted with an explosively-operated spin recovery parachute, and a slightly augmented test panel in place of the front gunsight, carrying an instrumentation time counter, altitude flashing red lights set at 8,000ft, test/cancel buttons for altitude lights and audio warning, turn and slip indicator, and aileron and rudder position indicators, sideslip indicator, parachute stream switches, live and release parachute indicator lights, parachute release switch, and a large incidence gauge, calibrated from +60° to −60°. A ciné camera was fitted to the rear cockpit, and was used during initial solo trials.

Over 350 spins were carried out by Andy Jones during four weeks of trials, and these confirmed the spin-resistant nature of the Hawk, an impression formed during the earlier stalling programme when

Above:

The original Hawk, XX154, was still earning its keep as a trials aircraft in 1978, and is seen here hauling pairs of 1,000lb bombs on the outboard stations and early-standard (with fins) drop tanks on the inner pylons.

harsh control misuse had never resulted in an incipient spin. He found that the aircraft could be spun off a straight stall, or off a turn, by applying full rudder, and moving the stick fully aft with neutral ailerons. The first turn was slow, but if pro-spin controls were maintained, the rate of rotation and IAS built up in the spin. Recovery was always obtained on centralising the rudder.

Various combinations of misused control sequence and partially applied controls were investigated during entry to the spin, invariably leading to increasingly unsteady behaviour, large variations in incidence, and sideslip. Recovery was always prompt by centralising rudder and tailplane. Similarly, many combinations of mishandled controls were investigated on recovery, but if the rudder centralised, the spin would always stop. Spins from grossly-mishandled aerobatics were investigated, but to provoke any departure at all full rudder was required, and recovery was prompt by centralising the controls.

It was at this stage of the flight development programme that the team at Kingston and Dunsfold began to feel that the Hawk was beginning to show the sort of potential as an advanced trainer, with considerable combat capability, for which it had been aiming from the very beginning. It was this performance and quite outstanding handling in combat manoeuvring, together with the already-obvious load-carrying and range capability, which led to the pilots putting forward forcibly their own views on the idea of a lightweight, single-seat combat

version of the aircraft. They were however disappointed that the standard of equipment on the Hawk for the Royal Air Force fell far short of what was readily available.

It was recognised that if the Hawk was going to follow the Hunter and other Kingston-developed aircraft in being sold to the air forces of the world, it was going to have to do so in the face of the most severe competition. Fortunately the company embarked upon the building of a demonstrator aircraft, registered by special arrangement with the Civil Aviation Authority G-HAWK, containing many additional features which, later on, were successful in proving that the Hawk was, without any doubt, the top contender in all respects in this very competitive world market.

It is also worth noting that the all-round flying qualities of the Hawk had been achieved in minimum time, and with minimal cost (the building at Dunsfold aerodrome which was the ground station for the telemetry links to the test aircraft was little more than a large garden shed bought by HSA for £38). Simple external 'fixes' on the aircraft were developed in traditional Hawker flight test methods. Deliberately harsh use of the flying controls in combat manoeuvres and gross mishandling could be demonstrated with confidence, and a stalling and spining clearance obtained.

One thing that the Dunsfold team made quite clear was that no such clearance would be sought until it was satisfied; too many trainers in the past had 'bitten back' after they had entered service. The Hawk had no speed limit for the pilot to observe, and it was demonstrated beyond any doubt by climbing the aircraft to the maximum altitude, and rolling over into a vertical dive at full throttle to achieve the maximum advisable Mach number.

Determined efforts were made to spin inverted, and it was found that in this case the rudder had to be consciously centred on recovery against a

60

tendency to blow on. Stall turns and recovery from the vertical with diminishing airspeed were also investigated, and it was found that the aircraft normally fell through to a vertical dive if the throttle was closed and the controls centralised. The engine put up with severe mishandling during the spinning programme and came out of it with credit. It was provoked to surge on only six occasions, under conditions of extreme angles of attack and sideslip, or both, together with large speed oscillations. The test flying showed that at normal instructional altitudes there was ample warning that conditions in the spin were deteriorating long before engine surge would be experienced in service.

Warm weather trials were carried out by Jim Hawkins with Hawk XX156 at Luqa, Malta in June 1975, and a total of 15 sorties were flown. Data was obtained on all aircraft systems under high-temperature conditions, and all aspects of aircraft and engine performance were examined. The cabin conditioning system had produced some mechanical problems prior to these trials, but in the opinion of Duncan Simpson the conditioning system, 'is quite the most effective yet produced on a Kingston-built aircraft'. XX156 was flown in Malta with maximum external stores configurations on four pylons and centreline gun installation, and on completing these trials it continued to Cairo where 10 demonstration flights were made for the Egyptian Air Force in several configurations. The return to Dunsfold was flown by way of Crete and Rome at the end of a demanding tour in terms of time schedules and weather conditions. A total of 34 sorties was carried out involving 39 hours of flying.

Trials in the weapon-training role for the Royal Air Force were continued at Dunsfold and elsewhere and included the jettisoning of Matra 155 rocket pods, both ballasted and unballasted, the jettisoning of CBLS pods, the dropping of 4lb and 28lb practice bombs, and the firing of Matra rockets. The 30mm Aden gun was fired at high and low altitudes, and at extremes of speed and G.

During this part of the test programme, the engine was cleared for unrestricted handling throughout the specified speed and altitude envelope. Cold and hot re-slam accelerations had been made from pre-stall buffet conditions to maximum IAS and Mach number, from sea level to 40,000ft, and with 5° of sideslip and in pushover manoeuvres up to minute 1G. Slam accelerations were also made on the final approach to land, and on the runway after touchdown with exaggerated nose-up attitudes. Cold re-lights on the engine were made with consistent success between 15,000ft and 25,000ft, from 250kt to 0.85 IMN, and hot re-lights were also obtained over the same envelope by 'catching' the engine on deceleration.

Drag measurement results from all the test flying showed substantial improvement on both specified and predicted values, and this emerged as a gain of some 15% on the original range performance figure. Encouraging climb and speed performances were obtained, and the thrust boundary and turning performance of the aircraft proved 'quite outstanding' Duncan Simpson concluded in a paper written for the Royal Aeronautical Society, in February 1976.

'It has already tested the stamina of all the pilots who have participated in the programme — sustained

Left:
Back at snowy Dunsfold after a warm tour of the Middle East in February 1978, test pilots Andy Jones (left) and Jim Hawkins clutch celebratory glasses of champagne. On the tour they took the Hawk through Egypt, Saudi Arabia, Muscat/Oman, Dubai, Qatar, Kuwait and Jordan.

values of over 7G have been recorded in level turns, and the intermediate altitude manoeuvrability is such that few modern combat aircraft are capable of remaining with it.

'The pilots who have been involved with the programme are confident that this aircraft will be a firm favourite with students and instructors alike. There can be no greater challenge than to replace the Hunter in the advanced and operational training role in the Royal Air Force. The Hawk will do this, and much more at a fraction of the cost, and will follow its famous forebear in other air forces in a variety of roles.'

HSA sent the Hawk, with Duncan Simpson and Andy Jones, to the Paris air show at Le Bourget in June 1975, and the aerobatic qualities of the aircraft were demonstrated before the public for the first time — 'up against' the Franco-West German Alpha Jet, with which it was competing head-on for sales in world markets.

Farnborough show 1976 was the next big public outing of the Hawk, and it proved to be a complete contrast to the restrained 'first-footing' of XX154 at the 1974 display. During the intervening two years the whole Hawk programme had geared up to such an extent that no fewer than nine of the new trainers took part in the flying programme on three of the days of the show, moving across the airfield in an immaculate close arrowhead formation, led by Duncan Simpson, and always spot on time, a considerable achievement, as this was a 'scratch' team, brought together in a short space of time.

The lead aircraft, painted in RAF camouflage, was XX156, the second off the assembly line, fitted with fuel tanks on the inboard pylons and Sidewinders on the outers — the first time that a Hawk had been demonstrated before the public carrying hardware. Immediately behind it came the company-funded demonstrator G-HAWK/ZA101, painted in two-tone brown desert camouflage, and then seven aircraft finished in the red and white of RAF trainers, and flown by a mixed bag of Hawker Siddeley, RAF and Boscombe Down pilots — including a couple of Americans on exchange. This 'scratch' formation team took off from Dunsfold each day it performed, started its run in to the Farnborough show over a roundabout near Odiham, and afterwards dispersed to several airfields.

Two months later, on 4 November 1976, came the big day of first deliveries to the Royal Air Force, with two aircraft ferried from Dunsfold to RAF Valley in North Wales. Duncan Simpson commanded the first, with Air Marshal Sir Rex Roe, Commander-in-Chief RAF Training Command, in the second seat. The air marshal in fact did most of the flying, but Duncan carried out the landing. This was because the weather conditions at Valley were foul, with black skies, torrential rain, and a strong, gusting wind. A soaked airman pushed the chocks under the wheels, then ran for shelter, and the pilots then went in   to face questions from a small press conference. Aircraft number two, commanded by Sqn Ldr David Young, the RAF project pilot at Dunsfold, with Air Vice Marshal 'Togs' Mellersh, Senior Air Staff Officer Training Command, in the second seat, arrived about an hour later, and at that point there was a celebratory glass of champagne in the officers' mess, and a warm welcome from the Commanding Officer, Grp Capt David Thornton, and his team of instructtors. The first delivery of a brand-new aircraft type to a Royal Air Force station does not happen very often, and this was a rather special occasion for everybody concerned.

Above:
First RAF pilot to fly the Hawk was Sqn Ldr David Symons, seen here (right) with Duncan Simpson after they had landed on this significant day, 11 September, 1974. This was immediately after XX154 had been brought back to Dunsfold by Andy Jones after its first appearance at a Farnborough show, with Duncan Simpson 'chasing' in the Hunter, and before it was grounded for the installation of test instrumentation. *BAe via Duncan Simpson*

6 A Trainer for the RAF

With first deliveries completed, the Hawk gradually eased into service with four Royal Air Force units — RAF Valley, for advanced flying training, RAF Chivenor and RAF Brawdy, for tactical weapons training, where the emphasis is on weapons delivery and fighter tactics, and the Red Arrows aerobatic team. By any standards the Hawk in RAF service built up an exceptional safety record, despite the fact that flying hours went up by 4,000 a month.

RAF Valley has the most Hawks on charge in the RAF and is responsible for accumulating over half of the Service's flying hours on the type. It has three training squadrons, all part of No 4 FTS, and there are two other Hawk units at the station — the Central Flying School, training Hawk instructors, and the Standards squadron. It is at Valley that the RAF's student fighter pilots receive their first taste of a high-performance aircraft, arriving at the base in Anglesey, North Wales after around 100 hours on the Jet Provost, with its side-by-side cockpit. Students rapidly become used to the tandem cockpit of the Hawk, with its superb field of vision, and they are then set upon an intense programme of flying during which the required standards are extremely high, for from initial entry into the RAF the student achieves his ambition of becoming a front-line fighter pilot only after 400 flying hours, and three years of tuition.

After learning the basic art of flying the Hawk, the students are subjected to a demanding and steeply-

Below:
Mechanics on the flight line at RAF Brawdy prepare XX192 for a sortie.

Above:
Brawdy Hawk XX105 looses off a salvo of Matra 155 rockets.

Right:
This grainy close-up of Matra 155 rockets leaving the pods is taken from a trials film.

rising learning curve which takes them through the syllabus of the advanced flying training programme. At RAF Valley they are grouped in courses of 10-12 each, with three courses run at each of the station's training squadrons. There can be as much as a 50% failure rate, but alternatively the whole group can pass to be awarded their wings. The next stage after Valley is to progress to one of the tactical weapons units, but not all of the newly-qualified pilots move in that direction towards their goal of fighter pilot. Some who are competent pilots, and yet do not reach the very high standards which are demanded of front-line fighter pilots, are redirected to multi-engine support aircraft training.

Back-up and support for the flying training programme at RAF Valley is provided by a large and efficient engineering wing. This is centrally controlled, and operates its own three first-line units, each of which deals with one or two squadrons. The wing names its units, rather than giving them numbers, so making them more personalised to the various teams which work on them. The three units are referred to as Sparrowhawk, which is responsible for maintaining the aircraft of No 1 Squadron and the Central Flying School; Goshawk, which looks after No 2 Squadron plus the Standards Squadron; and Seahawk, which deals with No 3 Squadron. Seahawk deals with one Hawk Squadron only mainly because it is located across the airfield and runway from the other two, and is therefore comparatively autonomous. But though it is smaller than Sparrowhawk and Goshawk, it is run on the same lines.

Maximum back-up maintenance and servicing on the flight line is provided for the squadrons by these three engineering units, but for specific problems each refers to the engineering wing's second line. This is divided into a number of different departments, each with its own specialists in specific fields, such as avionics, electrical, engine bay, hydraulics, and ejector seats, and is sited in the main complex at Valley. All Hawks, from whatever squadron, undergo the same scheduled maintenance and servicing programme. There are four regular patterns in the Hawk's routine servicing schedule.

At 150 hours there is the primary servicing, consisting of basic checks, lubrication, fluid changes and instrument accuracy checks. This is normally completed by a team of four men in two days, although the return of the aircraft to the flight line can be delayed in the (unusual) event of the rectification of serious faults, problem analysis or further in-depth servicing being required. The second service, at 300 hours, is designated as the minor. It comprises a more in-depth inspection of the aircraft, including structural checks, and a complete test of instrument accuracy. It also includes all aspects of the primary check.

During this check the emergency undercarriage stand-by cartridges are fired to test the system, and it is normal practice to change certain units, such as the undercarriage legs, for close inspection. Over 90 Hawk landings are logged at RAF Valley every day, and it is not surprising therefore that considerable attention is paid to the condition of the tyres, wheels and undercarriage. Primary and minor servicing are followed in turn by the primary star servicing, at 450

hours, and the minor star, at 600 hours. From this point, the sequence of servicing is repeated until the aircraft reaches 2,000 hours, when its first major servicing becomes due.

For the major, the Hawks were originally flown to No 5 Maintenance Unit, at RAF Kemble, but latterly the work has been carried out at RAF Abingdon. The service involves a complete strip down and overhaul. With the intensity of the flying at Valley, the Hawks soon reached their first major, and a number have been through it several times. On average, each aircraft reaches the 150hr flying mark in three to four months.

Because of the attention which was paid to accessibility in the early design stages of the Hawk — the design team set out to ensure that no component should have to be removed to get at another, a precept which had certainly not been followed in predecessor trainers — RAF engineers find the aircraft relatively easy to maintain and repair, and can ensure a remarkably quick turnround in between

Below:
RAF engineers work on the Hawk's Adour engine.

flights. The Hawk has a large number of rapidly-removable external panels and doors, and coupled with the aircraft's fairly low 'stance' on the ground, this allows much of the servicing work to be done without ladders and gantries.

The Adour is reached through the underside of the fuselage, and an adept team can remove it well within the hour. Its overhaul life span is about 1,200 hours, but some of the modules with which it is made up have a shorter span and are changed on a regular basis. After removal, engines are kept in the engine bay for up to eight days while being checked or having modules changed. Complete spare Adours are held at Valley, and these supply not only the Valley Hawks, but Hawks based at Brawdy or Chivenor, or at RAF Scampton, the home of the Red Arrows.

Valley also regularly services the Hawks' Martin Baker Mk 10 ejector seats. In the past these used to be overhauled twice each year, but experience has shown this to be unnecessary, and the period is now extended to 12 months. The ejector seat bay at Valley deals with six aircraft seat sets each month. Removal is simple, and most of the time is spent disconnecting the services to the seat, as well as disarming the three cartridges and rocket gun which, when fired, propel the seat about 300ft from the aircraft in seconds. After disconnection, the seats are unbolted and lifted out with a specially-designed boom crane.

RAF Chivenor, North Devon was reactivated after a break of six years to accommodate the Hawk, and the first flight was led there by Air Vice Marshal Peter Latham, Air Officer Commanding No 11 Group, in 1980, the AVM flying aircraft XX288. The decision to reactivate Chivenor as a fully operational training station from the care and maintenance basis on which it was placed in 1974 was taken in 1978 to meet RAF requirements for a second tactical weapons training unit to supplement that existing at RAF Brawdy, across the other side of the Bristol Channel, in South Wales.

From the time of that decision, Chivenor was the subject of an extensive modernisation programme, and with the arrival of the first Hawks, the second tactical weapons unit (2 TWU) was officially commissioned. Since then, the number of Hawks based there has increased to over 50, and the training programme is split between two operating squadrons, No 63 and No 1 (2 TWU), the latter's aircraft being distinguishable by having a letter painted on the tail, rather than a number. Both Chivenor and Brawdy carry out similar training programmes with Hawks, and as Chivenor's facilities were expanded, so Hawks from Brawdy were transferred there.

Both TWU stations also share the practice ground attack ranges on the South Wales coastline at RAF Pembrey. Student pilots posted to Chivenor arrive there after completing their advanced jet flying training with the No 4 Flying Training School at RAF

Above:
Underwing hardware on this Brawdy Hawk consists of Matra launcher, to starboard, and a CBLS (practice bomb carrier) to port.

Valley in Anglesey, North Wales, and during their stay, which lasts for four months, they are put through a very demanding course involving all the complexities of aerial combat, air-to-air gunnery, air-to-ground weaponry — including level bombing, dive bombing and ground attack — and tactical low flying, coupled with navigation.

The students are taught in progressive stages during the course until they have mastered all aspects of weaponry. The culmination of the course subjects them to a combination of objectives, which they must successfully complete before passing the TWU training. For example, a student might be told to find a primary target in company with another Hawk, carry out a successful attack, and then locate a secondary target, at the same time avoiding a third aircraft acting the role of an interceptor. Following the successful completion of the course, the pilots move on to their front-line fighter and bomber squadrons by way of the various operational conversion units (OCUs) where they are taught to fly the aircraft they are to serve with, such as the Harrier, Lightning, Jaguar, Buccaneer, Phantom and Tornado. With its active 'nest' of Hawks, Chivenor, which received its first RAF aircraft, a Hawker Hart, in 1935, is today an integral part of the Service's fighter pilot training programme.

RAF Brawdy received its first Hawks in December 1977, and the first students on the four-month long tactical weapons course flew them in July the following year. The Hawks of No 234 Squadron of the No 1 Tactical Weapons Unit at Brawdy provided the mainstay of the TWU programme until Chivenor was commissioned. Alongside No 234 Squadron was No 79 Squadron, with Hunters and a small number of Jet Provosts and Meteors, used for target towing. In 1981, the station was completing around 1,000 flying hours a month, and a planned reduction brought this down to about 890, shared between a complement of 30 Hawks and 40 Hunters. Brawdy's engineering staff totals some 800, consisting of 750 Service technicians backed up by around 50 civilians, many of them specialists from British Aerospace.

The Hawk as a trainer was graphically described by Wg Cdr Ian Dick, of the Air Staff at Headquarters Royal Air Force Training Command and a former leader of the Red Arrows display team, and Sqn Ldr Wally Black from the staff of the RAF Central Flying School, who was in charge of the Hawk project team which was responsible for introducing the aircraft to flying training at RAF

Top:

At the end of another day's intensive training, some 30 Hawks are marshalled on the flight line at RAF Valley.

Above:

Chivenor Hawks were 'massaged' neatly into this line-up for a publicity picture during 1982.

Right:

Proof of the much-vaunted view from the rear cockpit of the Hawk as a formation of five RAF Valley aircraft slides by. Photographer's gloves are on the coaming.

Valley. Extracts from Wg Cdr Diok's summing up in the *RAF Yearbook* are appended below:

'The Hawk is not only a superb aircraft, but also an excellent trainer. Its exceptional cockpit environment, coupled with its workload potential, and easy, yet challenging handling characteristics, make it the ideal training vehicle in which to teach the student exactly what the RAF wants him to learn. As one staunch supporter of the Gnat said as he climbed out of the Hawk after his first sortie — "Don't bother to wrap it up — I'll take two now".'

Most of the Hawk's systems management and emergency drills were simpler to cope with than those of the Gnat, the two officers concluded. There were no complications associated with flying the aircraft in manual following a hydraulic failure, and the ram-air turbine simplified hydraulic emergencies. The aircraft was easily handled throughout all emergencies, and practice forced landings were a straightforward exercise to fly.

As a training aeroplane, the Hawk's first noticeable advantage over its predecessors was that less conversion time was needed to learn how to fly it. The Gnat took a lot of time and practice to master its unique handling intricacies, whereas the same level of flying proficiency was more quickly achieved in the Hawk because it was simpler to understand, and easier to fly in the elementary respects. This saving in conversion time and continuation training meant that more syllabus hours than before could be devoted to the essence of advanced flying training — the applied exercises such as low-level navigation, close and advanced formation flying, all of which taught the student how to operate, rather than how to fly, the aircraft. A similar advantage applied at RAF Brawdy, where the tactical weapons unit introduced the ex-Valley student to basic weapons and tactical flying prior to operational conversion unit training.

Tactical weapons unit students who trained on the Gnat had the additional burden of coping with the demands of a different aircraft — the Hunter. With the introduction of training on the Hawk at Brawdy in 1978, this hurdle disappeared, with students already having the confidence that they could handle the Hawk, and so being able to concentrate their energies on learning operational flying skills. The training effectiveness of both RAF Valley and RAF Brawdy could only benefit as a result, because having spent more time on the applied exercises the students would inevitably be better-qualified when they arrived at the operational conversion units.

Right:
View from the rear seat during a
low pass over Dunsfold airfield,
where British Aerospace assembles
the Hawk.

Below:
This RAF T Mk 1 was loaned to
the manufacturer for appearances
at the 1978 Farnborough air
display. It carries early standard
100 Imp gal drop tanks (the fins
were deleted on later versions) and
Sidewinders.

But the Hawk went further than this as an effective trainer. One of the aircraft's outstanding features was that it was easy to fly when one wanted it to be easy, and demanding to fly accurately when one wished it to be a challenge. Consequently, the balance of training was greatly improved, and emphasis could be rightly placed on learning the skills applicable to later training and operational needs. This characteristic of the Hawk contributed significantly to the effectiveness of flying training, because it matched the RAF's training philosophy, which was to relate training precisely to the operational needs.

Also contributing to this philosophy was the Hawk's increased range and endurance which, compared with either the Gnat or Hunter, expanded its training capabilities markedly, and the limitations imposed by hour-long sorties applied no more. Composite sorties lasting up to $1\frac{1}{2}$ hours had been designed to include a number of exercises which involved flying further afield than before by both day and night. Thus flying demands and cockpit workload — to the right degree — could be applied to the students. This feature of the Hawk was of great training benfit, not only because it taught students operating skills to the right level of proficiency, but also because captaincy and airmanship qualities could be developed and tested to a far greater extent.

It was important to bear in mind that the requirements which had determined current flying training called as much for qualities of mental agility and quick thinking as they did for physical aptitude and co-ordination. Put another way, the modern, effective trainer was not necessarily one with a high performance in terms of speed, height or aerodynamics. It was more an aircraft with the potential to produce high cockpit workloads, and demanding systems management. Therefore, lack of experience on markedly swept-wing aircraft for ex-Hawk students was not seen as a shortfall in training prior to the operational conversion unit level.

The mystique surrounding swept-wing operations had now largely disappeared, since few modern fighters displayed the classic swept-wing characteristics of, for example, the Lightning, and it would be hard to find a greater cross-section of high and low-speed handling qualities in RAF front-line aircraft such as Buccaneer, Harrier, Jaguar or Phantom. Clearly, it was not possible for an advanced trainer to cater for this wide variety of aircraft performance, and it was up to the OCUs to provide the relevant type training.

On the Hawk in more general terms, Wg Cdr Dick and Sqn Ldr Black considered that the professional was more likely to be attracted to the Hawk's flying characteristics than its physical appearance. Lack of sharply-swept wings and a dolphin-like profile denied the Hawk the sharp, sleek, fighter-like appearance of its predecessors. Nevertheless, looks were not everything, and these particular features gave the Hawk two of its outstanding characteristics — an undeniably good lifting wing, and a superb view from

Above:
**Trials of Hawk with Sea Eagle were carried out during
1983. XX258 is seen here turning over** HMS *Glamorgan.*
The aircraft also carries drop tanks and Sidewinders.

the rear cockpit. The whole cockpit environment was
very comfortable and suitable for training, and
instructors and students alike were bound to enjoy
this aspect of the Hawk.

During the take-off run, rudder quickly became
effective at around 50kt and made directional control
simple. With a much wider tracked undercarriage
than the Gnat, the Hawk experienced no significant
or comparable effect from crosswind during either
take-off or landing, and it was during take-off that
one quickly discovered how well the flying controls
were harmonised. Light back pressure on the control
column got the nosewheel comfortably off the
runway at about 90kt, there was no difficulty in
holding the right attitude. With a very small attitude
change at 120kt, the aircraft left the runway cleanly
and was easily controlled, whilst the undercarriage
and flaps were retracted at a safe height.

As the aircraft climbed away from the airfield it
was immediately apparent that although the attitude
seemed very flat, the ground was receding at an
unexpectedly high rate.

Acceleration was as good, if not better than the
Gnat, and the climbing speed of 350kt was quickly
reached, and was anticipated by about 20kt for
adopting the climbing attitude of 12° or so. In these
conditions the initial rate of climb was better than
either the Gnat or Hunter.

About 10 minutes after brakes-off, the Hawk
could reach 40,000ft, and it was there that the
student was introduced to the effects of compress-
ibility, and learned about high-level manoeuvring. As
the aircraft accelerated from Mach 0.9 to 0.92,
differential shock waves over the wing produced a
difference between their centres of pressure, resulting
in a roll which required about half-aileron to hold
and correct. A familiar but mild 'cobblestone' effect
was felt between Mach 0.86 and 0.93, and minor,
random pitch changes could be discerned when
accelerating or decelerating between Mach 0.8 and
0.95.

Successful high-level manoeuvring — particularly
maxium-rate turning — required careful handling if
optimum performance was to be obtained — it was

Above:

Three RAF Valley Hawks turn in tight formation over the rocky coastline near their base.

all too easy to enter the buffet and lose speed. However, from a training viewpoint such demands were welcome as they offered a challenge to the student and a useful training yardstick for the instructor. Get it right, and the Hawk had a surprisingly good rate of turn at high level. For best performance the aircraft should be turned, just off the buffet nibble, at Mach 0.75 to 0.78. In this configuration the aircraft would turn tightly with a rate of descent no more than 4,000ft/min — a better performance than achieved by either the Gnat or the Hunter.

Get it wrong, by killing Mach with buffet or incorrect pitch attitude, and one lost turning performance very quickly. Moreover, to regain speed in this situation it was not simply a matter of releasing back pressure slightly on the control column; one really had to unload to recover the situation.

The handling techniques for entering a maximum-rate turn from high and low Mach numbers called for skill and good judgement from all pilots, but this was not the Hawk's only challenge. As height was reduced, so the handling characteristics changed. At around 17,000ft the best turning performance Mach number began to equate to the 360-370kt required for a 6G turn, and one had to adapt from the high level to the medium-level techniques. At lower levels one began to notice the lack of induced drag from the wing; excess thrust too was good, and an excellent rate of turn could be maintained through 360° with very little loss of height. For the best manoeuvring at the lower heights, speed should be kept up above 300kt and a delicate touch was needed to keep the aircraft just out of the buffet nibble — a fine sense of judgement.

Despite this requirement for a certain sensitivity, the Hawk was beautiful to handle, and acceleration up to Mach 0.88 at 10,000-15,000ft was an effortless excercise involving barely any attitude or trim changes. At medium level, 95% range speed was about 300kt, and it was here that one began to realise another outstanding feature of the aircraft — the remarkably low fuel consumption. Consequently range and endurance figures were appreciably better

73

Above:
The 30mm Aden cannon fitted to the majority of Hawks is the same dependable weapon which has seen service with other RAF aircraft types, including the Hunter and Lightning.

Below:
Weapons specialists at RAF Brawdy service the 30mm Aden cannon on a Hawk.

than for other trainers. The Hawk was easily capable of flying for $1\frac{1}{4}$ to $1\frac{1}{2}$ hours on a typical instructional sortie with enough fuel remaining at decision height for a 250-mile diversion — a significant asset from the flying training point of view.

The Hawk could be flown through a wide repertoire of aerobatics with spirited pleasure and few, if any, problems. Generally speaking, best performance was achieved by staying out of the buffet, although below 10,000ft very marginal buffet in the right places helped to tighten up an aerobatic sequence. With plenty of excess power, and such an excellent wing producing little induced drag, it was too easy to gain height, and power changes were necessary during aerobatics to match datum speeds and heights. Inverted flying was fully catered for in the Hawk, and tail effectiveness was more than ample for negative G enthusiasts. The Hawk was beautifully safe, with no aerodynamic vices to worry about during aerobatic exertions. However, from the engine-handling point of view, high rates of yaw should be avoided at low indicated air speeds.

Low-speed handling and spinning were perfectly straightforward, and presented no problems. The clean stall symptoms were easily recognised, and recovery was similar to the Jet Provost and, unlike the procedure with the Gnat or Hunter, involved unstalling the wing and re-establishing lift, rather than blasting the aircraft out with thrust. When gear and flaps were down, stall buffet was detectable through the airframe buffet, and recovery was straightforward and thoroughly safe. Indeed, the Hawk was very docile in the stall, and although there was some lateral instability, control was immediately regained once the stick was moved forward.

The Hawk was reluctant to spin or depart from controlled flight, even with gross mishandling of the controls. Nonetheless, students would be taught this exercise because of the valuable teaching points to come out of it. Once established in a spin, the characteristics were predictably safe. The recovery procedure of centralising the controls was immediately effective, no matter how the aircraft was spinning.

Left:
A Brawdy Hawk has one of its Matra 155 pods rearmed. Note Brawdy denomination on both pylon and pod.

The important teaching point for the student was that the Hawk spun differently from the Jet Provost, and the next aircraft he flew would probably spin differently again; the punchline was that, whatever the differing spin characteristics, the student must know the correct recovery procedure for the aircraft he flew.

The Hawk flew comfortably at low level throughout the useful speed range of 220 to 550kt. Lookout was excellent from both cockpits, and instrumentation was adequate for accurate pegging of speed and heading.

There was nothing unusual or difficult about flying the Hawk in the circuit. The instructor, overwhelmed by his unprecedented view from the rear cockpit, took a little time to adjust to the apparent nosedown attitude on the approach. Otherwise, circuit flying followed a standard pattern, with a downwind speed of 190kt, decreasing to 150kt by the end of the downwind leg, and 130kt straight in at the end of the final turn. The threshold speed was 110kt, plus one knot for every kilogramme of fuel.

On rolling or overshooting, the lifting power of the wing with full slotted flap was an experience to behold; the additional flap lift was supreme, and an impressive 1,000ft of height could be gained by the end of a 2,000yd runway. This was clearly where the flaps came into their own — as a low-speed aid; they were not designed for use in manoeuvring over 200kt.

Instrument flying was a simple process in the Hawk. The radar pattern was initially flown at 230kt, which was 30kt above the flap and undercarriage limiting speeds, but was more appropriate to advanced training. With gear and mid-flap selected, the speed was decreased to 150-160kt, and this was tapered to 130-140kt, depending on weight by decision height. Having landed the aircraft, stopping it — unasssisted by any brake parachute — required the same knack of braking technique used for taxying. 'Climbing out of the Hawk after one's first sortie, there is the compelling urge to get back in and do it all again.'

7 Red Arrows and the ETPS

The Royal Air Force's Red Arrows aerobatic display team re-equipped with Hawks for the summer season of 1980, retiring its ageing Folland Gnats, on which it had been formed in 1965, and which first flew as a type in August 1959. The team consists of 10 aircraft, nine of which participate in the displays, and one back-up, and basically the standard RAF T Mk 1 but with minor modifications, the most obvious of which is the array of three nozzles which inject a mixture of diesel oil and dyes into the jet efflux to produce the coloured smoke trails which are such an eye-catching feature of the team's performances. The diesel fuel is carried in a tank slung on the centreline pylon beneath the aircraft, which have distinctive liveries of bright red with a white cheat line running from the nose, down the fuselage, and forming the middle bar of the red, white and blue national colours on the tail fin.

The dashing paint-job matches perfectly the bravura style of the Red Arrows team in its heavy annual programme of around 100 shows each summer, both at home and overseas, but although each show appears heart-stopping to the hundreds of thousands of spectators on the ground below, they are meticulously choreographed and practised until near-perfection is reached. In this the team is assisted by its current mount, for the Hawk is a powerful but, at the same time, viceless performer, ideal for the advanced patterns which the Red Arrows trace through the sky, stressed for a lot of G, and smooth and certain when flying through the turbulent wakes left by its fellows. Team pilots like its air-conditioning and the fact that its cockpit is big enough to fit the largest man with comfort and is ergonomically advanced, with all the controls falling naturally to hand. Those who remember the Gnat do so with affection, but most now agree that the Hawk is a major advance in equipment, particularly from the maintainability of both engine and airframe, and from the range and fuel efficiency points of view. The

Below:

The Royal Air Force Red Arrows aerobatic team re-equipped with the Hawk for the summer season of 1980, retiring its Folland Gnats.

latter is of importance during the long-range ferry sorties which the Red Arrows are asked to carry out — such as flying from their base in Britain to Cyprus, in the eastern Mediterranean, for pre-season work-up in generally cloudless skies. Such a trip can be accomplished with the Hawks with only two refuelling stops, one in Italy and one in Greece.

The Red Arrows' Hawks are maintained by 80 ground crew, divided into two groups, one looking after the day-by-day servicing of the aircraft, including washing each one at least once per week, the other concentrating on the rectification of major faults and scheduled routine servicing. Nine men of the first-line group, led by the junior engineering officer, fly in the back seats of the Hawks to the air-

fields from where displays are to be mounted. Known as the 'flying circus', they provide an instantly-available back-up for the team, refuelling the aircraft and readying them for their performance. The remainder of the first-line team, some 18 men, arrives some 20 minutes behind the Hawks in a Lockheed C-130 Hercules, which also carries a range of support equipment, including a Land Rover, jacks, spares packs and the video camera kit which records every display the team gives.

Back at base between shows the first-line team checks each aircraft over every morning and then tows it out of the hangar to the flight line, where the nitrogen for the hydraulic system and the oxygen for the pilots are replenished. Usually the aircraft are fuelled before being hangared each evening. By the time the pilots have completed their briefings, the Hawks are primed to fly. Ground crew members remove the engine covers, check the safety of the canopy and the Martin Baker Mk 10 ejector seats, and then accompany the pilots on their walk-round

Below:
The sight that thrills hundreds of thousands of spectators each season: the Red Arrows break against a clear summer sky.

of the aircraft to make sure there is no damage or sign of leakages. The crewman then helps the pilot to strap himself into the cockpit and to close the canopy, and after the Hawk's auxiliary power unit has started the Adour he removes the chocks from the wheels. All nine ground crew then move across the apron in unison, pulling the chocks behind them, and receive acknowledgements from the pilots as they taxi out. The Red Arrows do almost everything like clockwork, including instantaneous starting of all nine aircraft, and they then take-off simultaneously in three formations of three, with rotation at 90kt IAS, and departure from the runway at 120kt.

The task of the second-line servicing team is to carry out jobs which are beyond the scope of the resources of the front-line team — mainly scheduled servicing, which is based on a cycle of 150 flight hours. After 150 hours, primary servicing is carried out on each aircraft, but minor services become due at 300 hours, and major work after 1,200 hours — and the trick is to juggle the flight schedules, with the use of the spare aircraft, so that these major works can be accomplished during the winter months. Away from the peak show season, some of the front-line team help the second line on major services. While a Red Arrows Hawk is out of commission a replacement is usually borrowed from other RAF units flying the type.

To even out the fatigue life on the aircraft (Hawks at the rear of the display formation tend to pull slightly greater amounts of G than those at the front

Special modification at the rear end of the Red Arrows' Hawks injects a mixture of diesel oil and dyes into the jet pipe to produce coloured smoke.

Close-up of a trials installation of the tank on the Red Arrows aircraft centreline which carries the liquid for the coloured smoke effects.

while maintaining position, while also using more throttle and airbrake) positions in the formation are changed regularly. Ground crew posted to the Red Arrows begin their career with the team in second-line servicing, moving into the first-line as and when vacancies occur. It is necessary to be dedicated to be a member of the Red Arrows maintenance team, particularly the front-line, for the hours and travel are extended, especially during the summer show season, and there is no extra pay — but despite these drawbacks, morale continues to be exceptionally high.

Red Arrows pilots generally remain with the team for a tour lasting three years, which means that each year three new men are selected and inducted into this very special form of flying. Usually there are some 30 applications each year for one of the three places, and these are reduced to a short list of 10, who then visit the team's base and stay with the existing members for a short spell. During that time, team members fly the aspirants in the back seat of the Hawks, both to get to know them and to 'get the feel' of their piloting qualities. Most of the newcomers have completed up to 2,000 hours on fast jets with the RAF before they are considered for a Red Arrows team place, and will have been assessed by the Service as above average — which is one place less than the top rating, 'exceptional'.

Apart from his flying qualities, the applicant will be rated for his 'clubability' — how he gets on with the other members of the Red Arrows, and for the impression he will make as one of Britain's ambassadors abroad. Colourful egomaniacs do not get far in the selection process, which is finalised by

the commandant of the RAF Central Flying School, of which the Red Arrows is a specialised detachment, and the leader of the team. The three new members are selected during the early summer of the season before which they are due to join the team, but during the current season they make some flights in the back seats of the Hawks during displays. After that, they go to the RAF station at Valley, North Wales for a conversion or refresher course on Hawks, including ground school and simulator flying, and during the autumn, after the end of the display season, they join the team as full-time members. Then starts the grind of polishing the pilots, and the aerobatic skills which they have learned with the squadrons, to the uniquely-high standard demanded by the Red Arrows. Firstly, a newcomer flies wing man with the team leader in a formation of two, learning how to keep tight station during manoeuvres. Then further Hawks are added, and the tyro is pushed further out in the formation so that position-keeping becomes progressively more difficult.

Then formation changes are introduced, after being explained in detail on a board on the ground before each sortie, so that the newcomers gradually learn each of the Red Arrows' patterns in detail. A video camera on the airfield constantly records each flight, and the films are played back as part of the debriefings so that pilots can pick out, and learn from, their slightest errors. By January the new pilots are usually integrated into the team, which then concentrates on working up its routine for the coming summer's season, including the honing of any new manoeuvres.

Each display which the Red Arrows give before the public lasts 20 minutes, and is carefully drawn up so that there is something to see during the whole of that time. The team has three 'shows', and which one is selected depends on the weather, or more accurately the cloud base. If this is at only 1,000ft, a truncated series of level turns is put on, simply showing patterns of formations. With the cloud base at 2,500ft, the team puts on a display restricted to rolling aerobatics only. With clear skies, or a high cloud base, the team demonstrates its full display, 20 minutes of breathtaking precision flying containing 15 different formations, a couple of dozen formation changes, 30 coloured smoke on/off commands and, while the team is regrouping out of sight of the crowd, five low passes in front of the spectator line by the 'synchro pair'. In this, two of the Hawks fly apparently head-on at each other, albeit safely missing each other by a carefully-predetermined margin. These passes include a spectacular barrel roll at 300kt, 100ft above the runway, and a slow pass with gear extended.

Then the seven others roar back over the heads of the crowd (the aerobatic manoeuvres are always carried out at a safe distance from the watchers) to go into more of the patterns — diamond nine, Concorde, feathered arrow, wineglass, carousel, parasol break. The laconic, clipped commands of the team leader come over the RT, expected and immediately accepted, as the Hawks pirouette with wingtips as little as 10ft apart. Finally the team comes in to land, one-by-one, in quick succession, to the plaudits of its fans and, on at least one occasion at the Farnborough air show, to a series of joke marks for artistic merit emulating those awarded in skating and dance competitions, held up on large boards on the balcony of the control tower.

Some $2\frac{1}{2}$ million people a year, it is reckoned, see the displays by the Red Arrows and their Hawks. It could be many more, for the Royal Air Force receives as many as 230 requests for a show each season at events as varied as open days at flying clubs and church fetes. Various yardsticks are employed in making the final choice of display venues. The safety of the site and its surroundings is of paramount importance, of course, but due consideration is also given to the impact of the team from the recruiting and RAF public relations points of view. During the winter months the Red Arrows further their public relations role by showing parties of visitors around their base and their aircraft, but in between, the grind of flying training goes on and on so that the team can continue to live up to the motto

on its crest — *eclat*, which translated from the French means brilliance.

One of the highest spots in the history of the Red Arrows was undoubtedly the team's tour of North America carried out during early summer of 1983. The 10 Hawks left their base at RAF Scampton on 3 May, each aircraft carrying a maintenance engineer in the second seat behind the pilot. Thirty other support staff, and the team Land Rover, spares, personal luggage and piles of publicity material, crossed the Atlantic in the less-glamorous environment of an RAF Hercules. It was the Red Arrows' second visit to North America, but the first with its Hawks, for in the original trip in 1972 its mounts were still the Gnats.

The team in 1983 was led by Sqn Ldr John Blackwell and consisted of Sqn Ldr I. Huzzard, Flt Lt J. R. Myers, Flt Lt T. W. L. Miller, Sqn Ldr E. H. Ball, Flt Lt M. H. DeCourcier, Flt Lt P. A. Tolman, Flt Lt S. H. Bedford and Flt Lt C. A. R. Hirst. The manager was Sqn Ldr J. E. Steenson, and the engineer Flt Lt M. E. J. Render. The tour itinerary read as follows: Scampton, Kinloss, Keflavik, Sondestrom, Goose Bay, Trenton, Niagara Falls, Patuxtent, Oceana, Andrews, Cherry Point, Charleston, Tyndall, Pensacola, Eglin, Randolph, Kingsville, Corpus Christie, Moody, Andrews, Anapolis, Bagotville, Goose Bay, Sondestrom, Keflavik, and home to Scampton. They were away for $3\frac{1}{2}$ weeks and during that time covered 12,000 miles, and flew 400 hours.

The journey over the Atlantic was done by the team aircraft in short stages from Kinloss, in Scotland, with refuelling in Iceland, Greenland and Labrador, and accompanied by a Nimrod. The first display of the tour was at Trenton, near Ottawa, and the biggest and most important at Washington DC at Andrews AFB, where the 200th anniversary of manned flight was being celebrated on Armed Forces Day. Official estimates put the crowds which turned out as around 700,000, while millions more saw the show on coast-to-coast television. That the Arrows 'wowed' the Americans there was little doubt, and the following morning the staid *Washington Post* gave its considered opinion that they had 'drawn raves'. The United States Air Force display team the Thunderbirds, in its F-16s, was also flying in the Andrews display, and the two teams had the opportunity later that same day to exchange notes at a reception given at the British embassy for the US hosts.

After its triumph in the nation's capital, the Red Arrows team took off south and west for more displays. At Charleston its audience was estimated to be around 100,000. On its way back, the team performed above the US Naval Academy at Anapolis, where it met its USN counterparts, the Blue Angels aerobatic team, which flies A-4 Skyhawks. The Arrows' performance had an added importance at this point, for by that time the Hawk had been selected by the USN for the training of future USN pilots under the VTXTS programme, and there were many senior American naval officers in the crowd who were having their first chance to assess their new aircraft.

The entire tour was a stunning success, and was summed up afterwards by John Blackwell, the leader, as follows, ' . . . the tour will stand out for years to come as one of the highlights of our time with the team. The tour was the most complex ever mounted by the Red Arrows in the team's 19-year history. Wherever we went, we encountered the fabled American hospitality, with everyone going out their way to help us make the tour a success. During the tour we had the unique opportunity to meet all three of the North American display teams, the USAF Thunderbirds, the USN Blue Angels and, on our return through Canada, the Snowbirds. Our British Aerospace Hawks, aided by some hard work from our ground crew, stood up well to their reputation for serviceability, and we were able to mount all our displays on time, without once having to use the spare aircraft. From the reaction we had from our American hosts, we believe our tour was a success. We hope that our displays showed our NATO allies that British technology and training are still amongst the best in the world'.

The Empire Test Pilots' School

Three T Mk 1 Hawks joined the aircraft fleet at the Empire Test Pilots' School (ETPS) at Boscombe Down during the summer of 1981. They were delivered from Dunsfold in primer and as standard aircraft, and were then flown to RAF Kemble for painting in the distinctive ETPS colours of red, white and blue. Back at Boscombe one aircraft was used for staff conversions and the second was sent to the hangar to be taken apart for re-instrumentation. The third aircraft was used as a back-up, but this was later to be modified as a variable stability aircraft, and is due to be returned in this configuration in January 1986.

Externally, the re-instrumented aircraft looks the same as the standard RAF Hawk apart from an air-stream direction detector mounted on the pitot head, and an OAT probe on the portside of the nose. Internally, however, there are major changes. In the cockpits, there is a visual indicator package located across the top of the coaming. It includes displays of control positions and forces, angle of attack and sideslip, and a relocated stopwatch. In the centre of the coaming display is an interchangeable fitting for the standard Hawk ISIS gunsight, a trial type spin panel, or a sensitive airspeed indicator and aneroid package for teaching performance flight testing.

Where the weapons control panel would normally be on the port instrument panel in the weapon trainer Hawk there is a fuel flow meter and digital fuel remaining indicator. And on the starboard cockpit wall there is a small panel containing instrumentation switches. The rear cockpit is similarly equipped with the exception of some master switches, while there is a second UHF radio which occupies the same relative position as that in the front.

The CCS (communication control system) is modified so that either pilot can use front or rear seat UHF or front seat VHF. ETPS Hawks have the extra UHF set to give provision for telemetry communications frequency. In the rear cockpit there are also further instrumentation boxes, and a cockpit voice recorder, located on the starboard console.

Within the airframe there is a modular data acquisition system (MODAS), which employs a digital tape to record various aircraft parameters, including control positions, air data, motion rates and engine settings. This tape deck is similar in concept to a domestic reel-to-reel, and is located in the space where the pilots' panniers would normally be stored. It can record the whole of a flight lasting up to 75 minutes, and samples the aircraft sensors 32 times each second. This information is then analysed, after the flight, by a ground computer, and is displayed in tabular or graphical format as a print-out by computer.

This sort of information is relayed to ground by telemetry for some high-risk exercises, such as spinning, and is displayed in 'real time' to a safety pilot at a visual display console. He is able to analyse what is actually happening to the aircraft at that moment, and can advise the crew of correct recovery actions. As is indicated elsewhere in this text, the Hawk has a natural reluctance to spin, and recovery is simple, but ETPS uses this safety factor by having a far wider spin clearance for its Hawks than is allowed by the limitations in the aircrew manual. As there would be need on real spinning trials to employ telemetry equipment, ETPS students have to be trained to use it.

The ETPS students, who are in fact highly-qualified pilots from Services in Britain and abroad, have inverted spinning included in their training programme. The Hawk was not originally cleared for this manoeuvre, and so the work was carried out in one of the school's Hunters. At the time of writing there were moves to have the Hawk cleared for inverted spinning, as the Hunters were rapidly ageing. A voice warning system is included, linked to the aircraft's spin panel presentation, and informs the pilot of safe recovery and ejection heights. The voice which passes such advice is that of Norma Ronald, an actress, replacing the bells and audio tones of previous systems, and her ultimate message is, 'If not recovered — EJECT!' A further difference in the ETPS Hawk to that of the basic T Mk 1 is a cassette tape recorder. It can be operated by either pilot, and is capable of playback during flight.

The Hawk is one of the first aircraft to be flown by students when they arrive at ETPS, and after brief dual and solo sorties they convert on to three or four other aircraft during their first month at the school, and a further three later on. The ETPS fleet includes, apart from aircraft already mentioned, Jaguar, Lightning, Basset, Andover, Lynx, Gazelle and Sea King. ETPS was established in 1943, during World War 2, to train test pilots for the British Services and industry, as well as foreign pilots based in the UK during hostilities, and therefore celebrated its 40th anniversary in 1983. Only the best of experienced operational pilots attend the rigorous $10\frac{1}{2}$-month courses, and selection is exacting in the extreme.

The variable stability (VS) Hawk, mentioned earlier, was developed by the Cranfield Institute of Technology to replace a Basset which was converted, also by Cranfield, in the early 1970s. The VS system on the Hawk is fully digital and can generate a far wider range of handling characteristics than the system in the Basset. It includes a reserve of computer power, enabling additional facilities to be added without extensive modification of the hardware. The VS Hawk is, in fact, an airborne simulator, and among its highly-sophisticated avionics are an artificial feel system, a digital simulation computer, a system controller, a flight safety monitor and primary flight control actuators.

Above:
One of three Hawks on the inventory of the ETPS taxies out.

The trainee pilot controls the Hawk indirectly by way of the artificial feel system and computer, while the controls of the instructor, or safety pilot, are linked physically at all times to the primary surfaces. The natural flying qualities of the host aircraft are electronically modified to simulate the instructor's requirements, and he is able to programme any linear of non-linear handling characteristics within the Hawk's flight envelope into the system. Through this system the feel of flying a series of aircraft can be given to the trainee — from the Tornado, with its variations of wing sweep, to a large transport machine like the TriStar.

Cranfield designed into the VS Hawk an 'intelligent' computer which monitors handling limits, and which introduces an automatic 'chop-out' when a limit is being approached. During the flight the instructor, or safety pilot converses with the computer, and this talks back to him by way of a multi-function cathode ray tube display which is situated in the centre of the instrument console. The instructor can, during a flight, introduce change in the aircraft parameters, and alter the stick feel. Side and centre controls are being introduced in the trainee cockpit, with the centre stick conditioned to reproduce any force gradient.

8 Hawk Sales to Foreign Air Forces

Above:
Early Mk 51 Hawks for the Finnish Air Force were assembled at Dunsfold, and later aircraft in Finland.

Finland was the first overseas country to buy the Hawk, choosing it in 1977 as its advanced weapons/trainer aircraft after a tough international competition in which the British-made aircraft was up against four other types, the French-West German Alpha Jet, the Swedish Saab 105, the Italian MB339 and the Czechoslovak L-39. Finnish pilots and engineers carried out a detailed and extensive evaluation of all the competitors during the mid-1970s, and when they finally expressed themselves completely satisfied with the Hawk they commented that they had been particularly impressed by its handling qualities at all altitudes, and under all flight conditions.

Further attractions for Finland were the low operating costs of the Hawk, its high reliability, its ease of maintenance, its low demands on manpower, its long fatigue life and its tolerence to extreme climatic conditions, especially the low temperatures in which the Finnish Air Force traditionally operates. And in its final adjudication, the FAF stated that a twin-engined trainer offered no significant advantages in reduced attrition or improved instructional capability over a single-engined aircraft.

The selection process by the Finns was completed during 1976, and a contract for a batch of 50 Hawks was signed on 30 December 1977 by the Finnish

Above:
Finnish Air Force Mk 51 No 302 turns over the Needles off the Isle of Wight during a test flight in 1980.

Right:
Mk 60 series export Hawk cockpit shows clearly the unusual amount of room for a trainer aircraft.

Defence Minister, Mr Taisto Tahkamaa, at the Solna, in Helsinki — once the home of the governor generals. The value of the contract was around £128 million, and there was intense satisfaction among the British manufacturers that their aircraft had broken so firmly into the export markets, for which it had shown such great promise almost since first flight.

The Hawk for the FAF was designated the Mk 51, so beginning the practice under which aircraft of this type destined for overseas are numbered above 50. But the contract was far from being a straight sale, for under its terms both British Aerospace and Rolls-Royce were committed to the establishment of industrial and commercial contracts between British and Finnish companies so that a substantial offset trade deal would be arranged, and new doors would be opened for Finland's own export markets. This was to be a 100% offset — that is, the value of Finnish sales was to be the same as the cost of the Hawks. The newspapers called the deal a 'swap', but BAe denied this, saying that it opened many new markets to Finnish industry, and also resulted in closer links and a greater understanding between Finland and Britain. Deals like this had been attempted by the British aircraft industry in the past (one Middle Eastern country had previously offered apples in part-payment for VC10s), but there had never been anything on this scale, and there were many people in both countries who expressed doubts that it could work.

However, after a great deal of hard work in unfamiliar fields by BAe executives, the targets and timescales set for the selling of Finnish goods were met and in many cases exceeded. Articles with unfamiliar trade names popped up in high street shops all over Britain, the classic case being displays of television sets from Finland in the Bentalls department store in Kingston-upon-Thames, a mile or so down the road from the BAe factory where the Hawks are made.

The main export drive from the Finns was to expand markets for their metal and electronics industries, and goods in these sectors made up the principal proportion of the reciprocal trade deals. A total of 72% went to these areas, a further 15% to timber and timber products, and a wide range of other products made up the remainder. Reciprocal trading deals covered such items as dockside container equipment, consumer materials, medical equipment, paper products, shipping, cable-making machinery and the TVs mentioned earlier. The

Saudi Arabia in 1978, and G-HAWK is on the sales trail. The picture was taken from a Royal Saudi Air Force Strikemaster.

remainder of the offset agreement went to the Finnish national aerospace company Valmet OY, which was to part-manufacture and assemble the majority of the Hawks destined for service with the FAF.

The first four aircraft were assembled and test-flown by British Aerospace at Dunsfold, and then handed over there to pilots from the FAF during 1980-81 for ferrying to Finland. From that point on, the remainder of the 50 aircraft order has been shipped to Valmet in the form of major 'knocked-down' items for assembly. Valmet has made the tailplanes, air brakes and flaps. By March 1984, the Finns had received 30 of their aircraft, and all deliveries had been either on time or ahead of schedule.

Hawks are replacing the Finnish Air Force's elderly Fouga Magisters, although the two types are to operate alongside each other until the FAF stands down the Magisters by 1987. Trainee FAF pilots begin flying on the 200hp piston-engined Leko-75 Vinka primary trainer. They then move on to the Magister, on which they complete 100 hours, before converting on to the Hawk. The future plan is to have them transition directly from the Leko-70 to the Hawk, and it was this policy which led the FAF, in the mid-1970s, to look for a new, modern, advanced trainer which was uncomplicated, rugged and straightforward to fly.

After completing their advanced flying and weapons training on the Hawk, the FAF pilots are then transferred to operational conversion units where they continue their training on MiG-21B aircraft currently in service with the FAF's front-line squadrons. The FAF Hawks differ in a number of details from the Mk 1s of the RAF, having the five weapons stations (instead of three) of all export aircraft of this type. The 30mm Aden gun pods on the fuselage centreline station which RAF Hawks normally carry in the weapons-training role were delivered for the Mk 51, but the Finns fitted their own VKT 12.7mm machine gun for training in ground attack and air-to-air combat. The aircraft also features a Saab gunsight.

Below:
During the 1978 Middle East sales tour, G-HAWK is
pictured at Almaza, Egypt loaded with five 1,000lb bombs,
one on each wing station and one on the centreline.

Bottom:
Landing back in the UK against a snowy background after
its 1978 sales tour, G-HAWK streams an original 7ft
diameter parachute, and carries early 100 Imp gal tanks
(130 Imp gal and 190 Imp gal are now available).

The Adour Mk 851 turbofan in the Mk 51 has the same thrust as the Mk 151 in service with the RAF, but has improved throttle response. The Finnish Hawks are also fitted with radio, navigational aids and cockpit instrumentation to suit FAF requirements, and the aircraft are also modified to accept the installation of Vinten reconnaissance pods, which can be fitted with both conventional reconnaissance cameras and infra-red linescan sensors. FAF Hawks are deployed in the Lapland Wing, and are based at Rovaniemi, and also with No 21 Squadron, at Pori, near the west coast, some 200km northwest of Helsinki.

Other overseas orders for the Hawk at the time of writing are Kenya (12), Indonesia (20), Zimbabwe (eight), the United Arab Emirates (24) and Kuwait (12). British Aerospace pressed the marketing of the Hawk hard in the Middle East, and the demonstrator aircraft was sent on an extensive tour of three countries in the area, during which it carried out 32 evaluation flights, including night operations, and weapons-delivery sorties. Weapons released included practice bombs, rockets and 30mm gun firing. A total of 20 guests was flown, and no sorties were lost through unserviceability — the only minor difficulties encountered being the malfunction of a gun, and the need to change a radio. Kuwait announced that it was to use its Hawks for similar purposes as the RAF — advanced flying and weapons training — but that they would have an additional ground-attack capability.

Half of the fleet of Hawks serving with the air force of Zimbabwe were blown up by guerillas while standing on their base airfield. The guerillas apparently broke through the surrounding wire and placed charges in the intakes of a number of aircraft, including four Hawks. One of these was a write-off as a result of the explosions, one was repaired locally, and two were sent back to British Aerospace in Britain for extensive repair and refurbishment. This was carried out at BAe's Kingston-upon-Thames factory, and the aircraft were then sent by road for final reassembly to BAe Dunsfold, from where they were test flown and then ferried back to southern Africa.

Indonesia, the furthest-flung Hawk customer at the time of writing, involves ferry delivery flights of 8,2000nm from BAe Dunsfold. Various ferry routes are followed, typically Dunsfold-Malta-Luxor (Egypt)-Dubai-Colombo-Jakarta, and the usual flight time is 18 to 19 hours. Crews are generally a mixture of BAe pilots and IAF pilots, their baggage stowed in the housing of the 30mm Aden cannon, blanked off for the occasion. Indonesia took delivery of the first of the initial eight Hawks which it ordered in 1980, and the first four of its pilots underwent conversion training with BAe at Dunsfold in the same year.

The Indonesians came back with orders for further batches of four Hawks to make their total number up to 20, the orders including spares and support. The second order, four four, covered the installation of smoke-generating units in the previous eight, and tail-braking, parachutes in all 12. The orders were signed in Jakarta by the Chief of Staff of the IAF, Air Marshal Ashadi Tjahjadi.

The aircraft has proved an outstanding success with the Indonesians, both on pilot conversion and operational weapon training, and in ground attack exercises have been the only aircraft in the IAF inventory to destroy successfully all of the targets allocated.

In the spring of 1984 hopes of Hawk sales to the Swiss Air Force were raised with the signing of a memorandum of understanding between British Aerospace and the Swiss aerospace company Pilatus for the joint manufacture of the latter's PC-9 turbo-prop trainer, should this aircraft be selected for the

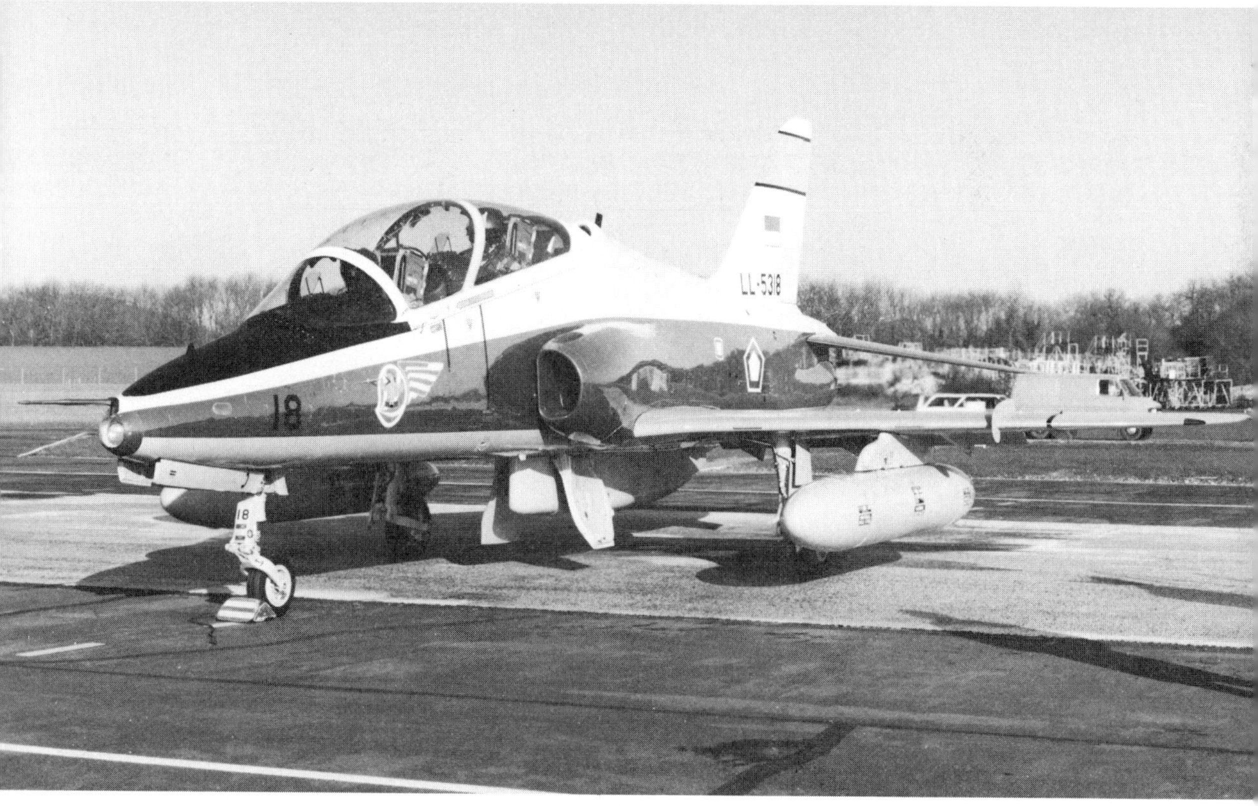

Left:
First four Indonesian Air Force pilots who underwent conversion training on to the Hawk at Dunsfold put their impressions on tape, with their first aircraft behind them. In the dark flying suit is Major Din Taka.

Top:
Nos 9 and 10 Mk 53 Hawks for Indonesia at Dunsfold shortly before being ferried to their home bases, a journey of up to 19 flight hours.

Above:
Eighteenth aircraft for Indonesia was delivered in red, white, yellow and grey colour scheme. Aircraft carries stretched 130 Imp gal drop tanks, and has the gun pod blanked off for the ferry journey.

Royal Air Force as a replacement for the Jet Provost. There was no commitment in the memorandum for the Swiss to take the Hawk, but it was considered highly likely that they would do so if the PC-9 deal, with a 50-50 work-sharing arrangement and final assembly in the UK, went through. British Aerospace pointed out at the time of the signing that Switzerland had been a good customer for British defence products since World War 2, having bought from the UK nearly 600 military aircraft, the Bloodhound ground-to-air missile, and the Rapier low-level defence system. BAe added that before agreeing the memorandum of understanding with the Swiss, it had made a detailed technical and commercial evaluation of the main contenders in the basic trainer field, notably the Brazilian Embraer Tucano, the Australian A-20 and the British Firecracker, and had concluded that, 'the PC-9 would provide the most cost-effective solution for the RAF's basic trainer requirements as a lead in to the Hawk advanced trainer . . . which BAe believes, with reason, is the best advanced trainer in the world.'

Three Mk 52s for Kenya turn in close formation over a mixed bag of aircraft on the ground. (From top to bottom) Hunter T8M with Sea Harrier radar in nose, Sea Harrier, Harrier GR3, Matador, Hawk T Mk 1 (RAF Valley colours), Hawk T MK 1 (RAF Brawdy colours), G-HAWK, Hawk Mk 53 for Indonesia, and Hawk Mk 51 for Finland.

9 VTX—Hawk Gets its Sea Legs

As early as 1975 British Aerospace became aware that the United States Navy had begun to consider seriously a successor for its elderly and thirsty T-2C Buckeye and TA-4J Skyhawk trainers, and that the Hawk could fit the bill. The USN anticipated that both aircraft, and the simulators that backed them, would have to be replaced by the late 1980s, and its Naval Air Development Center was instructed to examine the feasibility of the roles of the intermediate Buckeye and the advanced Skyhawk being played by one advanced aircraft, the programme to be labelled VTXTS — the V standing for fixed wing, T for trainer, X for experimental, and TS for training system. As this title indicated, the programme was to be a lot more than a simple buy of aircraft, and would include other systems — academics, simulation and computer-based training management and support. The prize was a massive one, consisting of a total contract worth approximately $5,500million, and 300 aircraft, with chances of further sales to the other US Services to follow.

By March 1978 the USN had awarded contracts for technology base studies for what was known as the undergraduate flight training system to four big US aerospace companies: Douglas Aircraft Co, General Dynamics, Northrop Corporation and Vought Corporation. These studies confirmed that VTXTS could be carried out by one aircraft of a type which would involve few technical risks, and in November that same year the Navy issued a memorandum which, in addition to reaffirming the validity of the VTXTS requirement, recommended the study of several alternatives with a view to filling that requirement. The alternatives were: the extension of the service life of the existing Buckeye and Skyhawk

General arrangement drawing, circa 1981, of the Hawk for the US Navy VTXTS requirement. The Hawk was chosen from among its competitors in November that year.

fleets, the modification of these two aircraft types, the acquisition of new-design training aircraft, the acquisition of existing modern training aircraft, and the use of a combination of these alternatives.

Among further VTXTS research started at around this period was a feasibility study to see if off-the-shelf aircraft could be modified suitably for operations off aircraft carriers, and as part of this, contracts were awarded to BAe for the Hawk, and to Dassault of France, and Dornier of West Germany, joint manufacturers of the Alpha Jet. The whole selection procedure was taking a long time, and to take the heat off the decision-making process the USN decided to extend the service life of its T-2Cs from 7,500 hours to 12,000 hours, and to bring back into service the retired T-2B to augment the number of intermediate trainers. In December 1979 the USN requested quotations for alternative system exploration, asking industry to propose total integrated training systems. Proposals were to include concept definition, training analysis and trade studies.

Ten proposals were received in March 1980. All of the US company propositions were for new aircraft. Three were for carrier-borne derivatives of existing European types — the Hawk, the Alpha Jet and the Aermacchi MB339 (from Italy). Each of the European manufacturers in the competition had, by that time, linked up with US companies, BAe's partner being Douglas, at Long Beach, California, within the McDonnell Douglas company. November

1980 saw VTXTS approved as a designated project, so that it broadened from an exploration to a full programme, with full-scale development to follow. Requests for proposals for full pre-full-scale development were released to industry in March 1981, and six proposals were received to develop system and sub-system specifications, prepare detailed programme plans, define risk reduction tasks, and perform key tasks prior to transition into full-scale development.

It was on 19 November 1981 that BAe heard that the Hawk-based system had won, the unofficial word having reaching Kingston during an apprentice prizegiving. The official announcement from the US Navy said that McDonnell Douglas had been selected as the prime contractor, teamed with British Aerospace to develop further the Hawk aircraft-based concept for VTXTS. And at the same time the USN awarded an engineering contract to McDonnell Douglas in anticipation of a pre-full-scale development contract award. It had been a long-drawn out fight lasting six years, and by that time the stack of paperwork which it had generated at Douglas alone stood a good 12ft high.

The Hawk, or T-45 as it is designated in USN service, won because the team of Douglas, BAe, Sperry Systems and Rolls-Royce were able to prove that it and its accompanying system would be able to save no less than 67% of fuel compared with training on the Buckeye and Skyhawk — enough fuel for 200

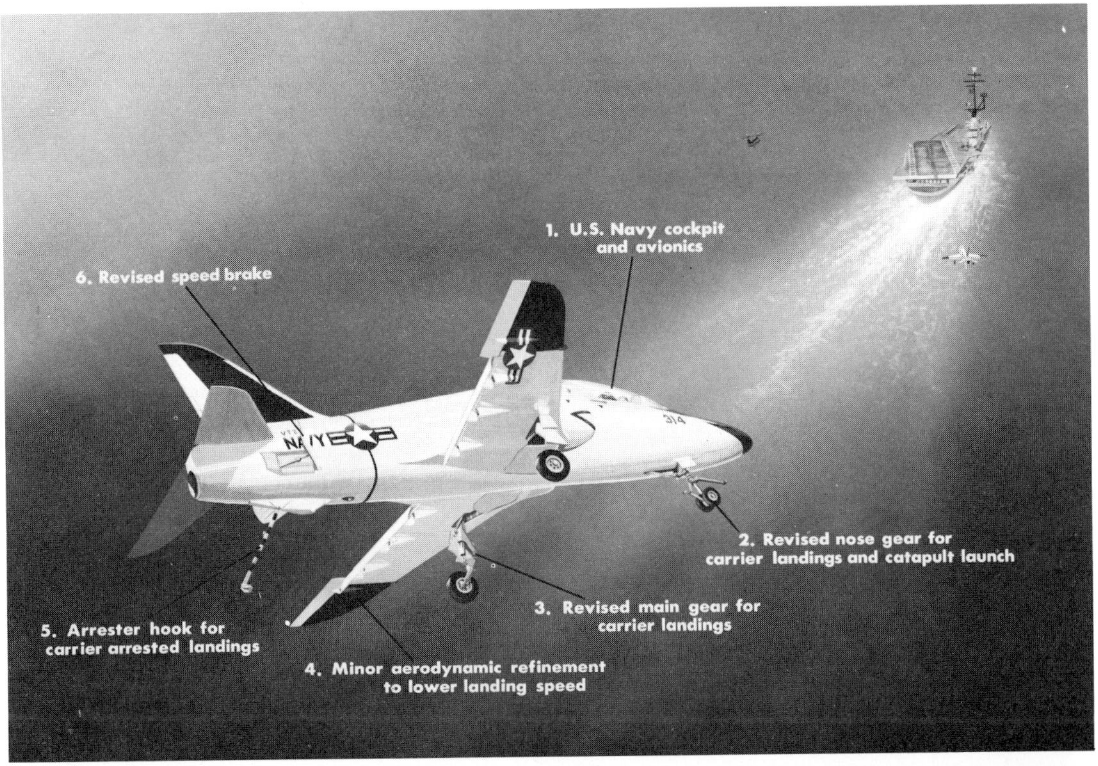

6. Revised speed brake
1. U.S. Navy cockpit and avionics
2. Revised nose gear for carrier landings and catapult launch
3. Revised main gear for carrier landings
4. Minor aerodynamic refinement to lower landing speed
5. Arrester hook for carrier arrested landings
NAVY

1 U.S. NAVY COCKPIT AND AVIONICS
2 REVISED NOSE GEAR FOR CARRIER LANDINGS AND CATAPULT LAUNCH
3 REVISED MAIN GEAR FOR CARRIER LANDINGS
4 MINOR AERODYNAMIC REFINEMENT TO LOWER LANDING SPEED
5 ARRESTER HOOK FOR CARRIER ARRESTED LANDINGS
NAVY

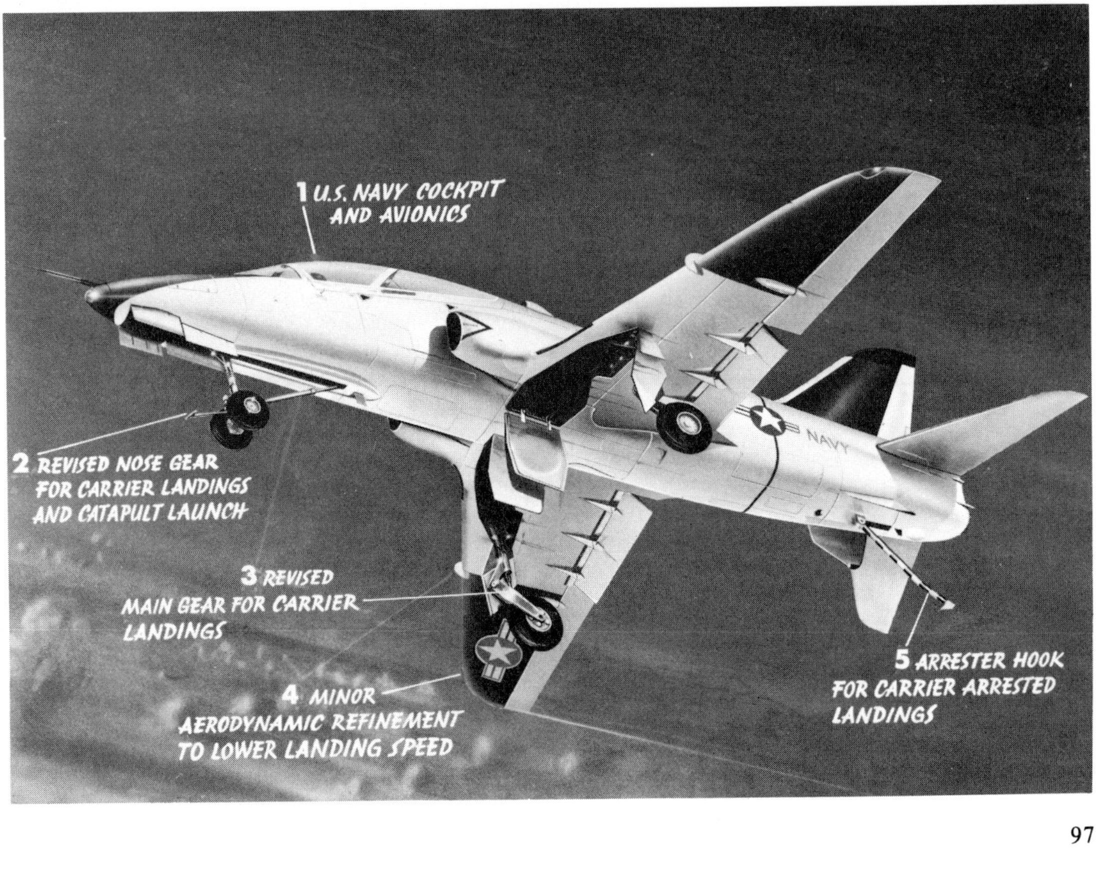

front-line jets for a year — would reduce the total cost of training each USN pilot by as much as 48%, would reduce flight hours by 29%, and would reduce support personnel by up to 46%, so releasing valuable manpower for redeployment to meet other service needs — and all this right through into the 21st century. The team had also been able to quote the excellent in-service experience with the aircraft of the Royal Air Force, and the fact that the Adour engine had, by that time, completed $1\frac{1}{2}$ million hours in service in Hawks and Jaguars, and the Japanese T-2 trainer.

The point was also made strongly that there was a lengthy history of aerospace collaboration between McDonnell Douglas and British Aerospace, the two companies having worked closely together since the early 1960s on three significant programmes — modifying F-4 Phantoms for the Royal Navy and the RAF, under a licensing agreement for 110 AV-8A Harriers for the US Marine Corps, and through the joint development of the advanced version of the Harrier for the US Marines (AV-8B) and the RAF (Harrier GR Mk 5). The Hawk case was also assisted enormously by two highly-successful visits to the United States by the company demonstrator aircraft G-HAWK/ZA101. The first of these was in May and June 1981, when during 30 days, in the hands of Jim Hawkins and Colin Roberts, the aircraft covered 10,000 miles in a highly-demanding tour of USN, USAF and USMC bases. The second was in April and May 1983, when it was based at Andrews AFB. The pilots on this occasion were Jim Hawkins and Taylor Scott.

During the 1981 tour — which was before the USN had announced its VTXTS decision — G-HAWK flew 86 guests, many of them important decision-makers in the Government and military, 10% more than had been originally planned. In all, the aircraft performed a total of 108 flights in 118 flying hours, including two transatlantic crossings. It made up to seven sorties in a single day, including solo aerobatic demonstrations. The demonstrator showed its capabilities right through the flight envelope, including simulated deck landings, using a USN mirror landing system, and non-flared touchdowns to show its compatability with carrier operations. It also proved its strength during the evaluation flights by pulling sustained load factors up to 8.9G, and 6G-plus in level turns. On each evaluation flight the Adour used on average between 1,100lb and 1,200lb of fuel, compared with the 3,000lb which would have been consumed on similar sorties by the USN's current advanced trainer. The influential observers noted that during this harsh itinerary, only one flight was cancelled, and that this high availability record was achieved with a back-up team which consisted of four mechanics, an electrician and a radio technician. The Hawk case was also impressively pressed home in the US during the spring of 1983 by the 15-day tour of USAF and USN bases by the RAF Red Arrows, mentioned in an earlier chapter.

Under the VTXTS agreement Douglas is the prime contractor, and BAe is a partner and principal sub-contractor for the airframe. Sperry Systems is

Below:

Graphic artist's impression shows a VTX Hawk sitting on the catapult ready for launch, while a second aircraft of the same type waits its turn.

Below right:

In flight on the US tour, G-HAWK and the back-up DC-9 formate.

also a partner and a principal sub-contractor for the simulators, while Rolls-Royce is a principal sub-contractor, for the engine. Turbomeca remains sub-contractor to Rolls on its part of the Adour. The US and Britain share 50-50 on production, but the final assembly line is in the US at Long Beach.

When the Hawk was originally selected as the VTXTS vehicle it was intended that all 300 aircraft should be what the Americans call 'carrier-compatible', that is, able to operate on to and off aircraft carriers, and be suitably modified to enable them to do so. But then, mainly to match the funding profile over the years, the concept of 'dry' and 'wet' Hawks was introduced. Wet Hawks were coded T-45A, and were to be fully carrier-compatible; dry Hawks — T-45Bs — would never go to sea, but would be used for practice landings and take-offs on airfields ashore. There were to be 54 T-45Bs, and they were to be shipped to the US directly from the BAe assembly line at Dunsfold, in the UK, with the balance of the 50-50 work and cost share to be readjusted between BAe and Douglas at a later stage in the programme. But the VTXTS programme has undergone many stresses and strains in the political and financial sectors of the US since 1981, and as a result of these the concept of dry Hawks has been dropped, so that all 300 aircraft are now back to the original concept of carrier-compatible.

Because it was only to practise mirror landings on shore stations without arrester wires, and therefore without the abrupt and heaving landings associated with such devices, the T-45B dry Hawks were to have been only lightly modified, with some strength-ening of the main undercarriage gear. This was to have been the main change, and other, smaller modifications were still in the discussion stage when this part of the project was brought to a halt.

In the case of the T-45A Hawk, the engineering changes are consistent with operating from aircraft carriers, although they do not alter the basic aero-dynamic shape or performance of the aircraft. The mods are mainly designed to deal with the immense strains placed on the airframe by firing it off carrier decks by catapult, and by thumping it down on landing with a vertical descent rate of up to 254ft/sec. The main landing gear is strengthened, as are the areas in the wings where the gear is attached. The nose-wheel and adjacent airframe is similarly treated, as this oleo not only has to take the full force of the sudden descent of the front of the aircraft after it has been jerked to a halt, but it is also attached to the shuttle of the catapult — and aircraft are hurled off the deck of USN carriers at the fearsome rate of from zero to 130mph in $2\frac{1}{2}$ seconds. Such force on an unmodified nosewheel leg would tear it clean out of the airframe. The single nosewheel of the Hawk design is replaced by twin wheels, and nosewheel steering is built in to assist manoeuvring on the small and crowded decks of carriers. An arrester hook is stowed beneath the tail, and the area of the airframe from which it is hinged heavily strengthened. Because the positioning of the hook clashes with the airbrake, this is deleted in the T-45, and a pair of air-brakes have been designed in a new position on either side of the rear fuselage.

The cockpit of the USN Hawk has numerous systems changes to meet US requirements for carrier operations, and also to give student pilots familiarity with the cockpits which they will fly when they graduate on to Fleet aircraft.

British-designed US10LV zero-zero ejector seats are installed, and the intermediate casing of the Adour engine is strengthened. To demonstrate the Adour's tolerance to catapult steam ingestion, a full-scale test was conducted with a Hawk at the Royal Aircraft Establishment, Bedford. The aircraft was parked over the catapult there, and the engine was run — faultlessly — through its entire rpm range.

Left:
This plastic full-scale replica of VTX Hawk for the US Navy has authentic twin nosewheel and arrester hook.

As indicated earlier, the T-45 Hawk is a part of the total VTXTS system, and the academics section is the first step in the building block process. Each piece of instruction in this section is designed to make the most of individual teaching tailored to the particular needs of each student. Teaching aids range from simple graphics to computer-assisted, and the aim throughout is to involve each student in the learning process, instead of leaving him to be a passive information recipient. Learning is self-paced, which reduces the amount of time needed from instructors. But although much of the instruction is automated, there are still a significant number of hours in the course where the students and their teachers meet 'eyeball-to-eyeball' in classrooms.

Simulation, where Sperry is the principal sub-contractor, is the second building block in VTXTS, aiming to develop specific cockpit skills to a level which allows time spent training in the air to be more productive. McDonnell Douglas' basic simulation philosophy is to train basic efficiency, and then to build up and validate that efficiency in training sorties with the aircraft. This ensures that valuable flight time is used in refining and integrating complex flying tasks, rather than learning elementary skills. Among the training devices being provided are instrument flight trainers, with a 6°-of-freedom plat-form motion system for instruction in cockpit orientation and instrument flight, and operational flight trainers, with a visual system giving a wide field of view, and a vibration motion cueing system. Pilots will be trained for all phases of the flight envelope on the latter device, which will provide three-quarters of their simulator training.

Winning the VTXTS contract against the intense competition of the aerospace industries of both Europe and the United States was the biggest break-through for the Hawk since its original selection to be the fast-jet trainer for the Royal Air Force in 1971. For not only was the programme itself a big one, but the follow-up sales possibilities within the United States were highly attractive. The US Navy could take a further 150, and the United States Air Force will want many hundreds of Hawk-type trainers eventually to replace its T-38s. Hawk sales will stretch into the next century, and there seems no reason why a version with limited re-heat should not emerge.

The VTX Hawk is scheduled to go into service with the USN in 1990, having made its first flight in late 1987 or early 1988, and so the British side was happy when a proposal was made to loan 12 RAF Mk 1 aircraft in 1984 for five years to the USN for under-graduate officer flight training. The aircraft were to be painted in USN colours, but BAe was to be retained as the prime contrator for supporting them. The loan had nothing to do with the VTXTS programme, being part of the deal under which Britain received ex-USN Phantom F-4Js to replace RAF F-4s serving the Falklands. The proposal was dropped before progressing very far on grounds of cost.

The announcement that the US Navy had awarded McDonnell Douglas, and its partners British Aerospace, Sperry and Rolls-Royce, a con-tract valued at $438million (£353million at the exchange rate at that time) to begin full-scale development of the T-54A training system came from Washington in early October 1984. McDonnell Douglas and BAe said that 300 aircraft were planned, with joint production between them, and with final assembly in Long Beach, California.

Under the terms of the contract two test aircraft were to be built, commencing in late 1985, with the first flight scheduled for late 1987. The two major partners added, 'Present plans call for work to begin on the first 12 production aircraft, along with associated ground-training systems, scheduled to be in operation with the Navy in 1990 at the Naval Air Station at Kingsville, Texas. The T-45A programme calls for Sperry simulators which rely heavily on the technology now used in the F/A-18 Hornet which Sperry is building for the US Navy. Many of the pilots trained in the T-45A will eventually be flying the F/A-18.'

By the time of the contract award, the name of the project had changed from VTXTS to T-45TS. It had been a long trail for the partner companies since the team was selected for the programme in 1981, but perseverance had paid off.

10 A Typical Hawk Test Sortie

Test-flying Hawks from the British Aerospace airfield at Dunsfold, whether the aircraft are newly off the production line, or have been in for modification or repair, involves countless hours of work from a small and dedicated team of test pilots and their flight-test observers. The work goes to a routine, but is never that, and is always highly-demanding. In this final chapter, a typical test sortie is described by one of the pilots involved.

The working day at Dunsfold, a few miles south of Guildford in Surrey, starts in the flying department with a briefing very much as it does in most flying units all over the world. Set in gently undulating country on the northern edges of the Weald, the airfield was carved out of farmland by the bulldozers of the Canadian Army in 1944 in preparation for the invasion of Europe. A memorial stone standing proudly in front of the pilots' offices, housed in the original wartime control tower, provides a lasting testimony to their efforts. After the war the airfield became a repatriation centre for prsioners of war and then resounded to the roar of heavy aircraft once again as Skyways took it over. In 1952 Hawker Aircraft became the tenant as the demands of jet fighter

Below:
Brawdy-based Hawk XX258 was loaned back to BAe to appear at the 1983 Paris air show. Aircraft is seen here carrying a real Sea Eagle — round No B12 — on the centreline, plus 190 Imp gal drop tanks and Sidewinders.

development, together with the expansion of Heathrow airport, forced a move from its field at Langley. The Hunter was followed by the Harrier and then the Hawk. All three aircraft are represented in today's briefing.

Hawker Aircraft gave way to Hawker Siddeley and it in turn to British Aerospace. Literally thousands of aircraft have been assembled, tested and flown here, all of them carving a niche in aviation history and all of them affectionately known as 'pilots' aeroplanes'.

Today's briefing follows the normal pattern. The weather is fine with a light wind from the southwest and scattered cumulus and stratocumulus. A front is moving in from the Irish Channel later in the day and will bring thickening cloud and rain in the evening. The diversion airfields are Farnborough and Boscombe Down. In the Channel, the Portsmouth danger areas are active and will need to be avoided. The briefing deals with the experimental aircraft first. There is a Sea Harrier to go to Yeovilton for ski-jump trials, another Sea Harrier being prepared for a missile firing, and a Hunter T8M on radar development. The two company-owned demonstrator aircraft, a Harrier and a Hawk with the apt registrations G-VTOL and G-HAWK, are both being prepared for demonstration flights later in the week, and a Harrier GR3 will be ready tomorrow for bomb trials. Others are in the process of modification or undergoing ground tests.

The production hangar anticipates a first flight on a Hawk Mk 63 for a Middle East customer and a final flight on a Sea Harrier for the Royal Navy. A T Mk 1 Hawk of the RAF which has been undergoing modification for the carriage of AIM-9 Sidewinder missiles is expected to be on flight test tomorrow. Two other Hawks are due to be ferried to the Middle East later in the week. Pilots are allocated to aircraft, together with flight test observers in the case of two-seat aircraft, and the day's programme starts.

My task is to take the first flight of the Hawk Mk 63, scheduled for 11 o'clock. My observer is Trevor Davies, Deputy Head of Flight Test Services, and a man whose experience of the Hawk goes back over 10 years.

We adjourn to my office to discuss the flight. My secretary greets me with the first post of the day — a depressingly large heap of paper covering a vast range of subjects from flight trials to proposed changes of airspace usage, engineering bulletins, visits by customers, overseas trips, lectures, development plans and so on. There are no apparent crises and the rest will have to wait. A test pilot in industry today can very easily spend all his time sinking under paperwork unless he disciplines himself to set his priorities and to attend first and foremost to the main task of testing aircraft.

This flight will follow a set pattern, developed in the course of testing over 300 Hawks and designed to prove the functioning and performance of every system. Engine start and control, radios, navigation aids, hydraulic services, back-up systems, performance and handling — all will be thoroughly examined and proven before the words 'Finished Flight' are written on the flight adjustment form, and the aircraft can be prepared for acceptance by the customer.

Below:
A mock-up of a British Aerospace Dynamics anti-radar missile was tried on XX338 during 1983.

Above right:
British Aerospace's private venture trials and demonstrator aircraft G-HAWK heads out to sea with an ADF aerial in the wing root on test. Picture was taken in 1978.

Below right:
Trial fits of the Stingray torpedo were carried out with G-HAWK during 1983.

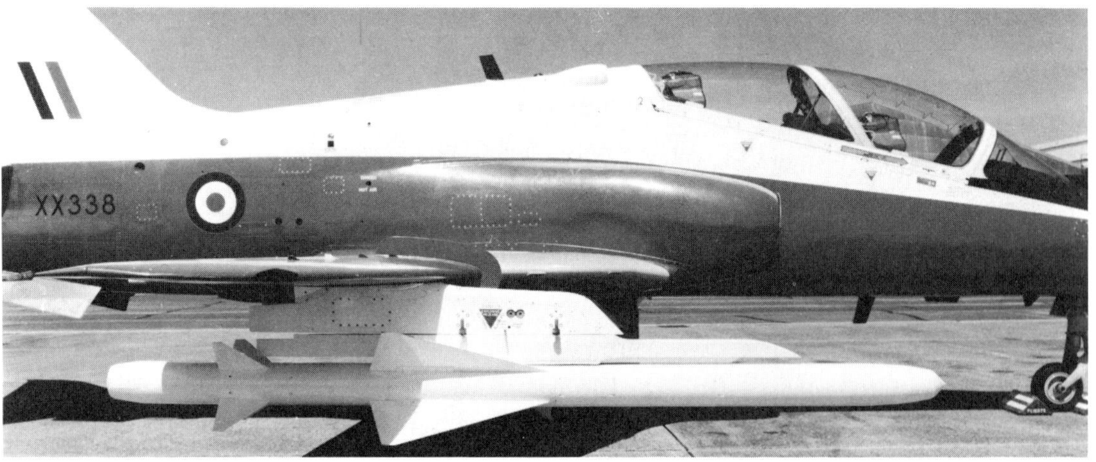

The phone rings. It is the hangar foreman telling me that the aircraft will be towed to the flight line in a few minutes. I ring Air Traffic to give the flight details and we go to change into flying equipment. It is the same as we use for the Harrier — a flameproof flying overall, stout boots to give protection against rocket blast if we have to eject, anti-G trousers which fit on over the flying suit and make one look rather like a cowboy, a lifejacket with a personal survival radio, and a very solid helmet with oxygen mask and a double visor — the inner one clear to give protection against a birdstrike which at high speed can destroy the windscreen and the outer one dark for use in the brilliant glare at high altitude.

We drive the half mile along the taxiway to the flight line where the aircraft is waiting. Production aircraft are unglamorous things, painted only in a peculiarly revolting matt yellow primer and with stencilled identification numbers sprayed on numerous panels and components at incongruous angles. When the flight tests are finished the engineers will remove almost all the access panels to make a final check that all is well and the aircraft will then be painted. The paintwork must be immaculate when the customer accepts his aircraft and so painting is the last item in the whole process of building, assembling and testing.

Even now after all these years there is something different about an initial flight; it's not a strong feeling, but rather just an awareness — no more — that this machine has never flown.

The external inspection of the aircraft is an essential preliminary to the flight. Only very rarely does one find any fault, but an open access door, an improperly fastened panel, a tool left in an intake, are all potentially dangerous and expensive, or at the very least extremely embarrassing.

The Hawk is refreshingly free of any need for ground power equipment so we are not plagued by the incessant roar of generator units which

dominates so many flight lines. The ground crew has positioned a broad set of steps by the cockpit, not only making it easy to get in, but allowing me a quick look at the upper surface of the fuselage to check that all is secure. The entire canopy hinges sideways so that we can get in by standing on the seats and then lowering ourselves gingerly down. A little care is needed here because the Hawk cockpit, like other larger fighter aircraft, is crowded with switches, controls and instruments and a clumsy movement can all too easily have dire results. Earlier versions of the aircraft had a rather exposed fire extinguisher button which had a habit of going off when nudged by a knee or a boot. The engineers always seemed to lose their sense of humour when faced with a loud whooshing noise indicating the drenching of the entire engine bay with noxious extinguishant.

After checking the Martin Baker Mk 10 zero-zero ejector seats we strap in. Nowadays the escape gear is prepacked in the ejector seat, and strapping-in is a far simpler business than it used to be when pilots had to carry their own parachutes out to the aircraft.

For a first flight the cockpit check is very much more detailed than for a routine flight. On this occasion it includes measuring the precise forces required to move controls and confirming the proper alignment and installation of every gauge — in fact inspecting the standard of assembly as well as the fact that all the switches and controls are set up for start.

My mind goes back to the time that this all started for me, some two years or more before the first Hawk flew in 1974, and the numerous discussions, debates, meetings and committees, sometimes frustrating, sometimes stimulating, that went to make up the design process. Ultimately aeroplanes, like any other man-made devices, are simply an expression of the ideas of the people who make them, and they carry an imprint of those involved — hundreds of widely different personalities from all disciplines ranging from engineers to military men, psychologists to pilots, aerodynamicists to politicians and civil servants. The cockpit as the nerve centre plays a vital role in determining the impression that pilots have of an aircraft. It has been gratifying to hear so many aircrew from air forces all over the world, with a background sometimes of British aircraft, sometimes French, often American, maybe Italian or Soviet, spontaneously declare after a short while at the controls how much they feel at home in the Hawk. All the argument and debate and effort and attention to detail has been worthwhile. And it continues. For it is fatal to stand still, to allow others in this fiercely-competitive world to steal a march and exploit new techniques to advantage.

The checks continue. The cockpit of this version owes its origins to that of the T Mk 1 which first flew all those years ago, but has evolved and will continue to do so, and the equipment list reads more like that of an airliner than of the fighters on which I was brought up. Twin VHF, twin UHF, VOR, ILS, ADF, Tacan, IFF, radar altimeter, duplicated altimeter and attitude indicators, horizontal situation indicators, fuel flow gauges, angle of attack displays — all sounding somewhat daunting and a little bewildering when written down yet all co-ordinated neatly and effectively in a way which lets today's pilot, even a student with limited experience, feel at home and confident in the complex world in which he has to live and work. The new technologies are even now bringing exciting changes which only a few years ago seemed more a part of the world of science

Far left:
G-HAWK hauls a load of 36 BAP100 anti-runway rocket bombs, made by Thomson Brandt, in this 1983 picture.

Left:
G-HAWK was flown in this configuration at the 1982 Farnborough air show — twin Sidewinders on the outboard stations, twin 190 Imp gal droptanks, and a reconnaissance pod on the centreline.

Below:
Turning above the clouds, G-HAWK shows off its load — on this occasion, during 1980, four 1,000lb bombs. These were trials weapons — full weight, but no explosive.

fiction than of reality. In a year or two the cockpits of future versions of the Hawk will be transformed by the use of multi-colour electronic cathode ray displays, a brand new and immensely capable weapon control system, a head-up display, and so on. Even that, one day, will have to be superseded if we are to remain competitive.

But that is in the future. It is time for engine start. A radio call to the control tower gives us the airfield data — pressure, temperature, wind — and we are clear to start. Fuel pump on, anti-collision light on, and a brief press of the start button puts the sequence in train. A small gas turbine starter unit , similar to the auxiliary power unit used on most airliners, begins to accelerate. Fifteen seconds later, a green indicator on the engine panel to the right of the main instrument panel shows that the GTS is up to speed, and the start master switch is moved to the start position. A valve closes, high pressure air from the GTS is fed to a starter turbine, and the Hawk's 5,700lb Adour, originally developed for the supersonic Jaguar fighter, begins to accelerate. Throttle forward to the idle position, and the engine lights up with a distinctly audible rumble. In a few seconds the rumble gives way to smooth running, and as self-sustaining rpm are reached the GTS automatically shuts down, the generator comes on line and the hydraulics, fed by twin high-pressure engine-driven pumps, reach normal operating pressure. Fuel flow stabilises at around 350lb/min, and it is time to switch on all the navigation and other avionic systems.

The checks continue. Electric trimmers, control movement, force measurements, weapons system and sight, navigation and communications, rear cockpit overrides, oxygen system and all of the standby and back-up systems. It is all very thorough and all very necessary.

It is time to taxi. The tower clears us to proceed to runway 25 and we begin to move. Braking and steering are provided by hydraulic brakes operated by foot motors on the rudder pedals. The brakes are checked in both cockpits and as we move slowly on to the main runway, cleared to backtrack to the take-off position, we run through the pre-take-off check and the safety brief. Canopy fully locked, ejector seat safety pins out, harness secure, central warning system clear and so on. Nothing much has changed here over the years whether the aircraft is a Tiger Moth or a Concorde. This is the moment when the flight is to begin in earnest, when the aircraft is to go through the metamorphosis from a cumbersome machine on the ground into a graceful creature of the sky. The ground is not this creature's environment — rather more its enemy. During take-off, energy is poured into the machine and, as it accelerates, the time available to deal with emergencies rapidly evaporates. It is an essential discipline before every take-off to remind oneself in advance of what the actions will be if problems arise. A few seconds of anticipation are infinitely valuable.

This Hawk has a brake parachute which can be used at speeds up to 160kt if necessary, and at the far end of the runway is a safety net which can safely catch and arrest the aircraft at up to 120kt. If the worst comes to the worst, the ejector seat can be used at any speed and height, even on the ground.

The aircraft is lined up for take-off and air traffic gives take-off clearance: 'Hawker Juliet (the callsign I have used since I came to the company in 1970) surface wind 250° 10kt — standard departure runway 25 — you are cleared for take-off'.

Below:
Cruising in the sunshine in 1981, G-HAWK shows off its red and grey/white 'US Navy' training markings.

Below right:
In this 1982 configuration, G-HAWK carries as Vinten recce pod on the centreline, drop tanks and Matra rocket pods.

I move the throttle fully forward and the engine accelerates rapidly with a momentary characteristic resonant howl as the rpm increase. Five seconds later we have full power, the rpm and temperature governed by an engine control amplifier and the fuel flow reading around 4,000lb/min. A quick check that the central warning panel is clear, brakes off and the Hawk accelerates quickly. Nose gently up at 100kt, and the aircraft lifts gradually at 120-125kt, after a ground roll of only 1,600ft or so. Brakes on, gear up and a steep noise-abatement climb takes us up at nearly 30°, putting us at 2,000ft by the end of the 7,000ft long runway. Power back to 80%, a gentle turn right to a heading of 280°, and we level off at 2,000ft to await hand-off to Farnborough ATC which will control our departure to the west below the airline traffic from Heathrow and Gatwick. Twenty miles to the south I can see the Channel beyond Selsey Bill and the Solent.

I hold the speed back to below 200kt for a check of the undercarriage. It is always the first item on the test schedule with a newly-built aircraft. I press the button to lower the wheels and start the stopwatch. The indicator shows three red flags as the gear travels, one to show each leg is unlocked. Eight seconds later, three reassuring thumps are accompanied by the indicators changing to green. We accelerate now to the gear limit speed of 200kt, check the rear cockpit controls, and raise the landing gear. All is well, and we accelerate for the next test at 450kt.

'Hawker Juliet you are identified on departure at 2,000ft! (ATC has received my IFF on radar and my aircraft's height is printed on its radar scope). 'Clear to call Farnborough Stud 4.'

The UHF radio has 20 preset channels for the most commonly-used frequencies, and every other UHF frequency in use can be dialled up if needed. We change to Channel 4 and call Farnborough.

'Farnborough this is Hawker Juliet on departure from Dunsfold, heading 280° maintaining 2,000ft.'

'Hawker Juliet Roger. Maintain 2,000ft. Turn left heading 250°. Avoiding action. Traffic is a helicopter right o'clock.'

We turn left and see the helicopter at about five miles a few hundred feet below.

'Farnborough Hawker Juliet is steady 250°. Are we clear to maintain heading and height for 60 seconds?'

'Juliet affirmative. Call when ready for climb.'

At 450kt I reduce power to hold the speed, and carefully trim the aircraft to fly hands off. We note the exact trim positions, angle of attack and other data, and compare the instrument indications between both cockpits. Trevor Davies in the rear cockpit notes the need for a small adjustment on the aileron trim.

'Farnborough. Hawker Juliet is ready for climb'.

'Hawker Juliet Roger you are cleared to climb to Flight Level 450 (45,000ft). Turn right 290° and advise passing Flight Level 100.'

I set full power and adjust the speed to 350kt. Trevor notes the instrument readings every 5,000ft. The Hawk climbs rapidly, particularly with the new Mk 861 Adour, a more powerful version of the engine fitted to the RAF T Mk 1s, and the earlier Mk 50 series aircraft. We call Farnborough passing 10,000ft, and are handed over to London Military Radar. The usual cheerful greeting follows, and we settle down to the routine of the flight. The gliding centre at Lasham in Hampshire passes behind us as we head towards Salisbury. Over to the left the Isle of Wight shows clearly against the background of a silvery sea, and the French coast is clearly visible beyond. Five minutes after starting the climb we are passing 30,000ft. Oxygen flow is normal and all looks set for the complete flight. While Trevor notes his data, I start to check the various navigation aids.

'London Hawker Juliet are we clear to turn left towards St Catherine's Point (on the southern tip of the Isle of Wight) to position for sonic run?'

'Juliet affirmative. Turn left 150°.'

Above:
**Prototype 130 Imp gal drop tanks are carried in this 1981
picture. The lines where the extra sections have been
grafted into the old 100 Imp gal tanks are faintly visible
fore and aft.**

As we climb higher the sky above becomes a
deeper blue and we can see further and further.
Passing 40,000ft some eight minutes or so after starting the climb, we are now flying on Mach number
rather than airspeed, maintaining a figure a little
above Mach 0.7. The rate of climb has now fallen to
about 2,000ft/min, and will reduce further as we get
higher.

Now as we cross the Solent we have a magnificent
view. There is no cloud over the sea, and the Cher-
bourg Peninsula shows clearly to the south. Further
away, the Channel Islands can be seen sparkling like
huge jewels, the sun glinting off the myriad of
glasshouses. Far, far below, the Channel is alive with
traffic, the sea lanes clearly showing streams of ships
of all sizes leaving their herring-bone wakes spread-
ing out behind them for miles.

Approaching 45,000ft, the cabin is very quiet and
most of the noise comes from the cabin conditioning
and pressurisation, pouring hot air into the cabin. It
is hard to realise that on the other side of that thin
canopy lies a blast of air at around -60°C.

'London Hawker Juliet is level Flight Level 450.
Awaiting dive clearance.'

'Juliet Roger. Maintain heading. You will be
cleared to dive in approximately two minutes.'

St Catherine's Point falls astern. We have to be
well clear of the coast before being cleared by
London to supersonic speed to ensure that no
damage is done ashore.

'Hawker Juliet you are clear to dive. Advise
supersonic and subsonic.'

I roll the aircraft inverted and, pulling gently back
on the stick, put the aircraft into a dive of about 60°.
The speed builds up rapidly. At Mach 0.88 there is a
quite clear shuddering, rather reminiscent of driving
a car along a cobbled road. At Mach 0.92 there is a
slight tendency to roll, easily corrected with fairly
coarse aileron, and as we pass 0.94 all the buffeting
and shaking stops. The Machmeter quickly passes
1.0 and then steadies at 1.18. The aircraft will not fly
any faster — it is held at this speed by its own drag. I
recall the period when we first suspected that the
Hawk would be able to achieve supersonic speeds. It
was not originally designed to achieve such feats, but
the very advanced wing used a design technique of
which there was not a great deal of experience, and
all the forecasts were conservative — very conservative as it turned out. It took a long time to con-
vince our designers of the astonishing result they had
achieved.

At supersonic speeds the Hawk remains respon-
sive. Passing 30,000ft in a near vertical dive, the
pressure in the cockpit is rising rapidly and my
eardrums give me a clear message. We are descending at over 1,000ft/sec — it is time to pull out. A
gentle back pressure on the stick, the 'G' rises to +3
and the dive slackens. The anti-G suit inflates,
squeezing the lower half of my body like an over-
affectionate python, and the speed begins to slow. At
Mach 0.94, as the shock waves over the wing move,
the aircraft increases 'G' to about +5, and moments
later we have started to climb again, the run completed. Trevor puts a tick against the item on the
flight test schedule and records the speed achieved.

The next test is cabin depressurisation at 35,000ft.
Not a popular item, it involves switching off the

108

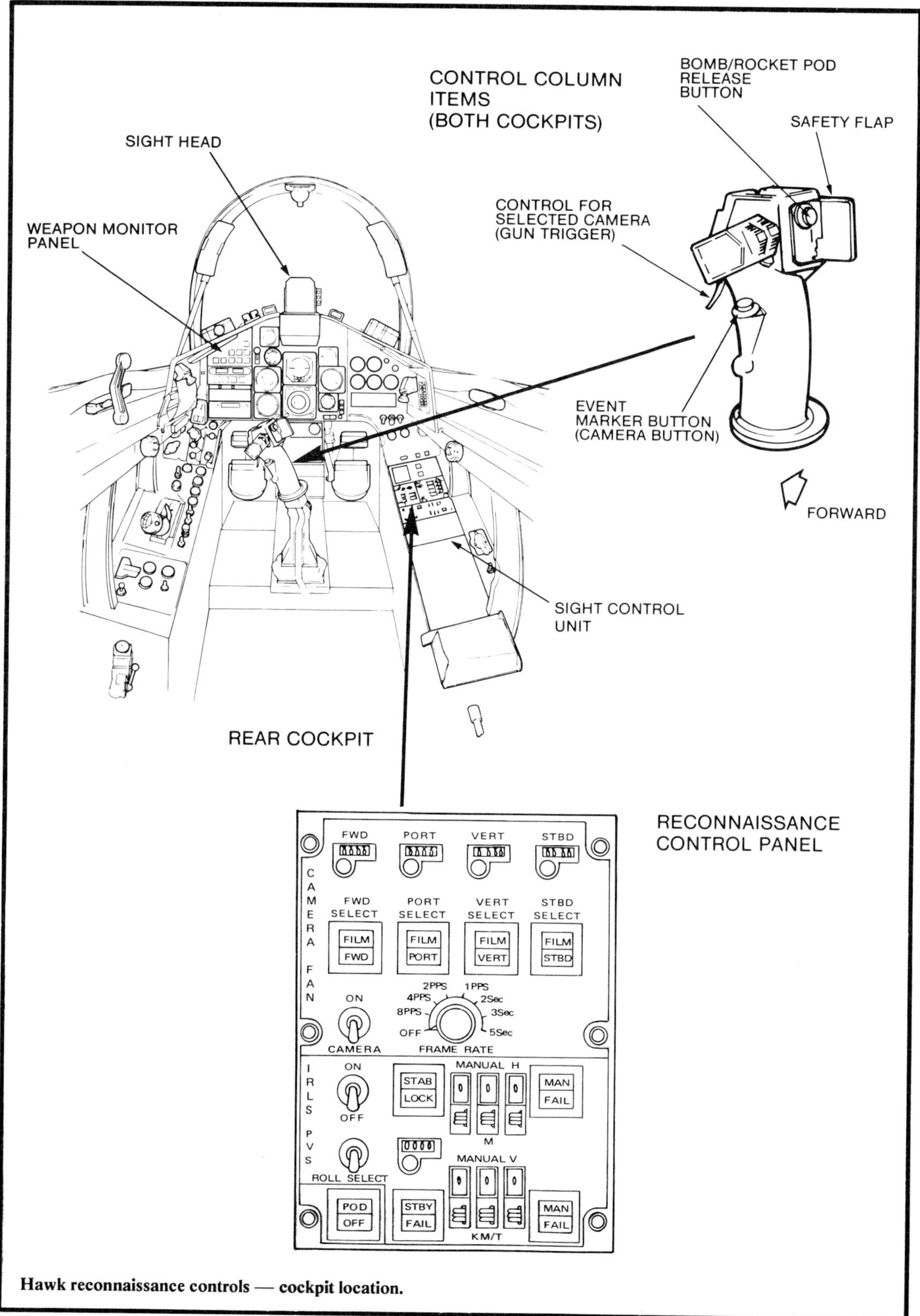

Hawk reconnaissance controls — cockpit location.

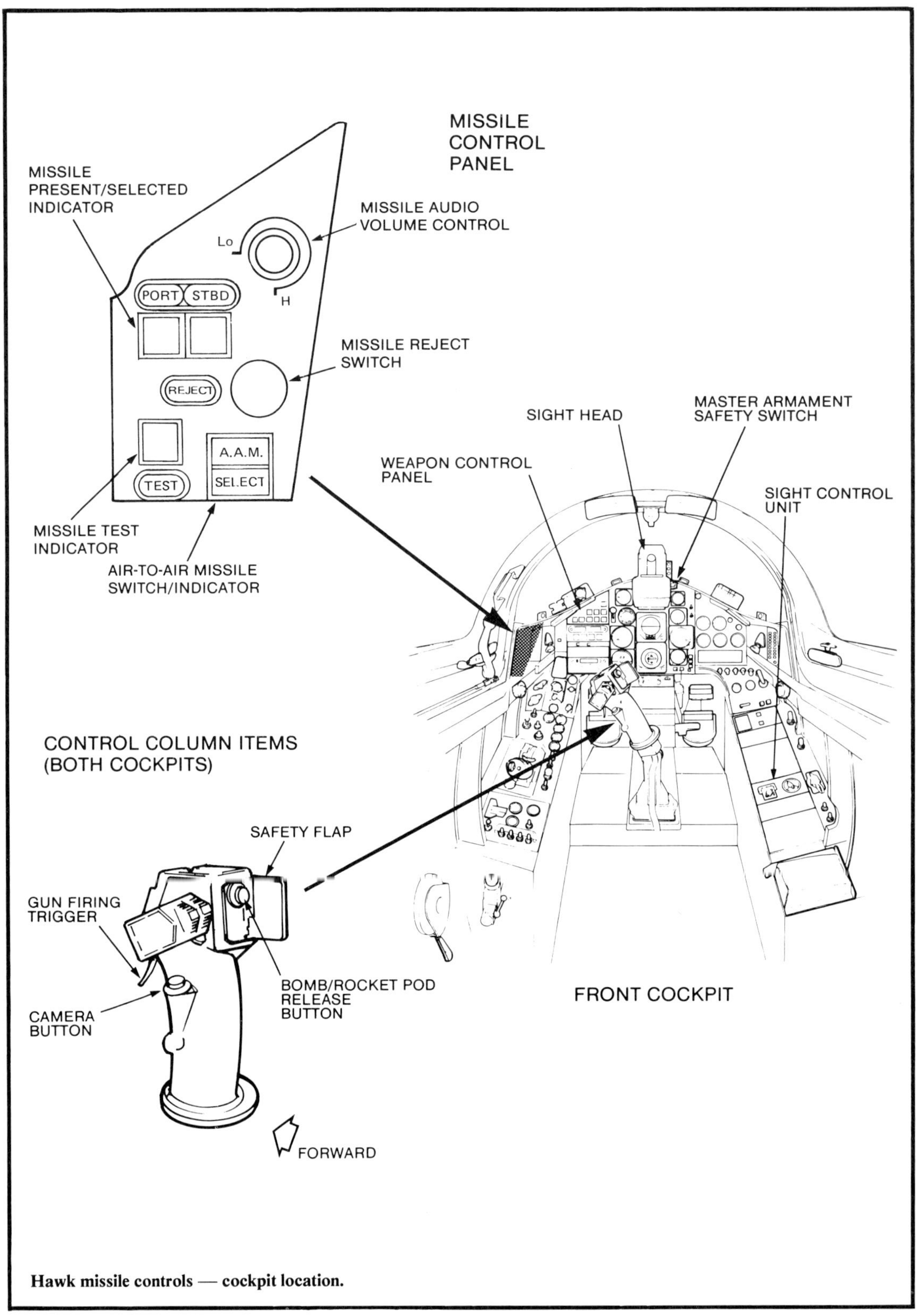

Hawk missile controls — cockpit location.

pressurisation to check that the warning system operates properly. We check our oxygen and tighten our masks to the emergency position. A brief countdown and then the system is turned off. Cabin pressure falls very rapidly, equivalent to a climb over twice as fast as the descent we have just made. My eardrums feel as though they will rupture and I hold my mouth inelegantly wide open to let the air out of my lungs and help the eustachian tubes from the ears clear. Air hisses out of the tear ducts at the inner edge of my eyes. The cockpit fills with mist as the pressure falls and then cabin pressure warning: a red caption on the warning panel accompanied by flashing red 'attention' lights on the coaming and a loud siren like an angry police car. Enough of that. I put the switch back on and everything returns to normal with a rush.

Sundry minor tests follow — an engine acceleration check at 30,000ft, an airborne light-up of the gas turbine starter, to confirm its operation in its secondary role as a back-up relight system for the engine, a trim check at 15,000ft and it is time to stall.

We normally do this at 10,000ft, and it still astonishes me how very slick this aeroplane is. It takes a long time to slow down.

In the descent towards 10,000ft we are handed over to Boscombe Down Control, since it has a lot of traffic in the area we will be using. We are cleared to begin our tests with a minimum level of 8,000ft. Below us the air is busy with helicopters from the Army base at Middle Wallop and a variety of aircraft from Boscombe. The radio chatter is a mix of accents from all over the world as the students from the Empire Test Pilots' School go about the business of learning their trade.

The first stall is to be in the 'clean' configuration — wheels and flaps up, airbrake in. We note the fuel state so that the precise aircraft weight is recorded, set the power at 70% and begin the slow deceleration. The nose rises almost imperceptibly as the speed falls, and the angle of attack tells me what we are asking of the wing. Just the faintest burbling at around 9° AOA, the Hawk loses speed faster, and then at 10-11° a pronounced buffet and shaking. Control is still excellent and finally at 14° the aircraft drops its nose slightly and very slowly rolls off to the right.

The next stall is in the landing configuration with the undercarriage down and full flap. Power is set at 85% to simulate the landing approach. This time the speeds are much lower thanks to the powerful flaps, and the stall comes at about 95kt. This time we see a rather marked roll-off as we approach the stall, and Trevor makes a note to have the precise setting of the flaps checked.

Some systems tests follow — emergency hydraulic pump, fuel and oil pressure warnings — and now it is time for spinning. As we climb rapidly to 30,000ft for the tests, heading now towards the Bristol Channel with the Brecon Beacons showing beyond, I recall the spinning trials. Of all the trials done on the Hawk before its release to service, these were for me the most interesting. The work was hard, often with over 20 spins per sortie, each one the subject of discussion with the ground safety team which had a telemetered set of aircraft data played out in front of it as the trial was proceeding. In all we did something like 600 spins, and at the peak were doing around 70 to 80 each day. No wonder I couldn't walk straight at the time. So right was the design of the aircraft that not a single modification had to be made as a result of that exhilarating programme.

We are at 30,000ft now, and back under London Control.

'Hawker Juliet cleared to spin. Minimum altitude 15,000ft. Traffic is a tanker with four chicks at 10,000ft westbound. Advise entering and recovering.'

We enter a turn to the right, checking straps tight, flaps up, airbrake in, throttle idle. At 160kt I put on full right rudder and pull the stick right back. The aircraft shudders and rolls to the right, the nose dropping rapidly. The rudder pedals shake violently and a lot of force is needed to hold on full control. The instruments tumble in an apparently random and meaningless way, and we are in the spin. The motion is deceptively lazy but the altimeter shows we are descending at about 500ft/sec. The recovery is always reassuringly quick. Rudder and stick central and within a second the rotation stops and we begin to pull out of the dive.

Next comes the part which still astonishes most of the pilots who fly the Hawk — the turn to maximum 'G' at 500kt. As we dive down to 20,000ft, the speed builds up rapidly, and with full power set we start to turn. At a crushing plus 8G the rate of turn is very high indeed and it is all I can do to hold up my head. The G suit presses fearsomely on my legs and stomach, but without it this sort of manoeuvre would be impossible to tolerate. Amazingly, the speed only decays very slowly, and after a complete 360° turn we are still showing 450kt.

Next comes the check of maximum level speed, and for this we fly down to the south coast, pasing Selsey Bill on our left and heading past Littlehampton towards Beachy Head. Full power selected, and the fuel flow settles at 4,500lb/min. The engine is governed at its maximum temperature of 640°, and the speed builds up more slowly now as we near the maximum. A cross check between front and rear cockpits, and we note the stabilised value — 560kt or over 640mph.

We slow down, and crossing the coast northbound we call Dunsfold for recovery. One or two tests remain, and the 20 miles to the airfield is soon eaten up. The landing will include a check of the brake parachute and the brakes themselves.

On the downwind leg, once the speed is below 200kt, I lower the undercarriage and the flaps. The added drag reduces the speed and power is increased to 85% or so. I let the speed reduce until the angle of attack rises to the right value for approach — $5\frac{1}{2}°$. A crosscheck of speed shows 118kt, and this is the speed we will have at the runway threshold. A small reduction of power as we turn on to the final approach, and the Hawk descends at about 1,000ft/min.

Clearance to land is given, and moments later we touch down, streaming the brake parachute as we do so. Nosewheel down on to the runway and then the tremendous tug from the 'chute. Full brake now and seconds later the aircaft stops after a ground roll of less than 500yd. I jettison the 'chute, noting the time of landing, and taxi back to dispersal. The flight has taken 1hr 25min — these initial production test flights almost always take the same time — and apart from a few minor adjustments the aircraft is in good shape.

I still find it a miracle that after all the thousands upon thousands of man-hours of work, all the way from the mines where the metal ores are wrested from their repose of untold millions of years, through the mills, machine shops, the assembly line, the whole aircraft can come together so well.

One day no doubt we will look back on what we presently think of as a great achievement and laugh at ourselves for our presumption. But for now another Hawk has joined a growing fleet, ready to play its part in the history of the customer nation.

Hawk T Mk 1
Cutaway Drawing Key:

1 Pitot head
2 Landing lamp
3 Nosewheel compartment
4 Nosewheel door
5 IFF/SSR aerial
6 Forward equipment bay
7 Access door
8 Nosewheel leg
9 Towing lug
10 Shock absorber
11 Nosewheel
12 Rear nosewheel door
13 Radio and electronics compartment
14 Air intake
15 Front pressure bulkhead
16 Curved one piece windscreen
17 Instrument panel shroud
18 Rudder pedals
19 Electrical cable duct
20 Control column
21 Throttle
22 Gunsight
23 Canopy, open position
24 Canopy miniature detonating cord (MDC)
25 Headrest
26 Student pilot's seat
27 Entry step
28 Retracting step
29 External fuse panel
30 Rudder pedals
31 Control column
32 Instructor's gunsight
33 Instructor's windshield
34 Rocket launcher pod
35 Starboard wing pylon
36 Headrest
37 Instructor's seat
38 Throttle
39 Air intake
40 Rear pressure bulkhead

41 Oxygen cylinders
42 Air conditioning plant
43 Starboard wing fuel tank
44 Leading edge wing fence
45 Access panels
46 Vortex generators
47 Starboard navigation light
48 Glideslope aerial
49 Starboard aileron
50 Starboard flap
51 Ram air intake scoops
52 Heat exchangers
53 Anti-collision beacon
54 Fuselage bag fuel tank
55 Intake duct construction
56 Intake trunking
57 Fuel system access panels
58 Engine intake face
59 Ram air exhausts
60 Gas turbine starter
61 Starter exhaust
62 Ram air turbine doors
63 Emergency ram air turbine (extended)
64 Flying control rods

65 Skin doubler plate
66 Hydraulic reservoirs, port and starboard
67 Fin root fairing
68 Tailplane cooling intake
69 Tailplane control rods
70 Fuselage top diaphragm
71 Rudder control rods
72 Tailfin construction
73 UHF/VHF aerial
74 Dielectric fin tip
75 Rudder honeycomb construction
76 Rudder hinge control
77 Trim tab control
78 Rudder tab